Tramp Artist

Thelma Webb Wright

Tramp Artist

The Life of Robert Webb, Jr.

— ❧ —

Thelma Webb Wright

Tramp Artist
Thelma W. Wright 2003

Library of Congress Cataloging-in-Publication Data
Wright, Thelma
Tramp artist : the life of Robert Webb, Jr. / Thelma W. Wright
p. cm.
ISBN 0-9623650-1-7

Front cover art:
Courtesy of Colonial Williamsburg, Williamsburg, VA

Back cover art:
Courtesy of John and Mabel Ringling Museum of Art, State Art Museum of Florida

Photo credits:

All photographs in *Life in Cà d'Zan* (pp. 19–40))and *Glimpses of Cà d'Zan* (pp. 193–196) by Giovanni Lunardi and Terry Shank–Images courtesy of The John and Mable Ringling Museum of Art, the State Art Musem of Florida.

All photographs in *Glimpses of Williamsburg* (pp. 197–200)–Images courtesy of The Colonial Williamsburg Foundation.

Robert James Webb, Jr.

*This book is dedicated
to Bob and Rosa who gave me
the gift of life
and taught me how
to live it.*

R obert (Bob) Webb, Jr. was born in Methuen, Massachusetts, on May 25, 1897.

Conditions during his childhood were cold and harsh; work was all there was. He met a scruffy old painter at the age of fourteen. As he watched the man paint, his face frozen to the window of a vacant storefront, something happened. Young Bob knew in his soul what he wanted to do. He quit school. He wanted to paint.

By his twenty-first birthday Webb already had worked with several well-known artists, first under apprenticeship to F. M. Lamb, a famous New England artisan, for painting and restoration, and a year later on loan to John Singer Sargent for the Boston Library. Under less than auspicious beginnings, even as he endured staggering hardships, Webb's incredible talent emerged like the tip of an iceberg.

Circumstances led to his work on The Restoration at Williamsburg, Virginia, and at the Ringling estate in Sarasota, Florida. The family moved many times as he bounced back and forth between jobs, jobs which required his flexibility and range of talent.

Robert Webb gives us a slice of Americana. He was a unique character with loads of stories to tell: plain-speaking stories that can move one to laughter and tears. Between these pages is captured the constitution of a self-made man, an artist whose contribution is part of America's heritage.

Thelma Webb Wright

October, 2003

Contents

Tramp Artist

The Life of Robert Webb, Jr.

1963

A Man Observed

Love him or hate him,
Robert Webb was true to himself.

Best Friends: Bob and Tippy

 guide at John Ringling's home, Cà d' Zan, remarked to me, "We know your father's work, but we don't know the man."

My first thought was, "There's an awful lot about the man you don't need to know!" Then Dad's own words came to me, "What's wrong with the truth?"

My name is Thelma Webb Wright, and I devoted hours in contemplation of writing about my father, Robert James Webb, a man who was so complex, so talented. I was baffled until one day I had the realization: the book will write itself! Dad created it through his life–and I merely needed to document the events recorded in letters he had written, newspaper articles, tapes, and stories told by family and friends.

In writing about my father I relived the events with a full range of emotions. Often I had to stop typing to wipe away the tears or have a good belly laugh. I grew in under-standing, acceptance, and love of a man who didn't do anything in an ordinary way.

Honestly, there had been times in my life when I hated him, times when I loved him, and times when I did not understand his actions. Then there were times when what he said or did was so insightful and humbling I could not bear it. As I live my life, my knowledge continues to grow in realizing that this man–artist, husband, father, grand-father–left each of us a priceless legacy of memories.

Love him or hate him, Bob Webb was true to himself.

Source Material

"There are so many people involved with a structure like this. No one man can say *I*. You say *we* because *I* alone means nothing. It means nothing in anything."

–Robert Webb, Riverside Baptist Church, Jacksonville, Florida

I, alone, could not have completed this book. It has been a nine-year labor of love, completed with the help, encouragement, and guidance of many people.

Many connected with Colonial Williamsburg in Williamsburg, Virginia contributed:

Cathy Grosfils and Marianne Martin at the Visual Resources of the John D. Rock-efeller, Jr. Library. Stephen E. Haller of Archives and Records. Philip Moore–still work-ing in the Paint Shop–recalled my father as his teacher. Also from the Paint Department: Bruce Marquardt, Vernon Hubbard, and Bruce Wildenberger all contrib-uted stories.

Ron McCarty–at The John and Mable Ringling Museum in Sarasota, Florida–has been the long-time registrar of Cà d' Zan. He gave precious time guiding me through Cá d' Zan to show me detailed art work by my father.

David Weeks, the author of *Ringling, The Florida Years* and Mrs. Charles Ringling Lancaster contributed valuable information.

I want to acknowledge the kind cooperation of the following:

The Boston Public Library, The Virginia Museum of Fine Arts, The Riverside Baptist Church (Jacksonville, Florida), The Bellamy Methodist Church (Gloucester, Virginia), and Christ Church (Montclair, New Jersey).

I am indebted to many friends: Joan Underhill, Dinny Bondybey, Peg Berntson, Jim Slaugh, Pat Johnson, Ann Cecil Renick, Joan and Robert Coogan, Sy and Jill Fein-gold, and Frances Buschur, who designed the cover.

Special thanks to Dr. Paul Runge, who guided me to Tom Biddle, an editor who, with patience and skill, performed a miracle with my manuscript.

Life Begins

It was a tough country in those days.

Hannah, Bob, and Robert, Sr. (1900)

*M*y name is Robert James Webb, and these are the words I spoke to my daughter, Thelma, when she asked about me and my life a while back. There is a lot I could have said and a lot that I didn't say, but everything in this book is the truth as best I can remember it.

My Family

James was my maternal grandfather's name. My ol' man was born in Kent, England, in 1852. He was brought up in a thatched-roof house, one big room with a fireplace at one end, and a dirt floor. They'd chop up straw and use cow manure for plaster, mix it up and make blocks for the walls. My father had five brothers and one sister. There were two cows in the house–on top of where the cows were was a platform with a ladder. Kids slept upstairs over the cows.

The farm next to my grandparents had three kids. Their house caught on fire and burned. The old folks died and left three kids, so my grandmother took them in and raised them. They were given the name Webb, as simple as that. Named them Webb.

My mother, Hannah Maynard, came from Liverpool. She was short and stout. She had three brothers. Liverpool had a city-market square where poor parents sent kids to be sold to big estates for work. The butlers of these estates would go there, look them over, and bid on them. My mother was sold to be a skivvy maid.

My mother was paid two and six pence a month and lived on the estate.

My parents came over from England on a ship named Grecian Monarch. *It was a combination coal heaver–you heave coal with a shovel, so they called it a combination coal heaver and sailing ship. In those days, the British government didn't like the younger people leaving England for what they called the New World. They did everything they could to keep them from coming, made their lives miserable. They'd be glad to get rid of the old people, but they wanted to keep the young people.*

Everybody was so damn poor that the only way they could get here was in a village lottery. Families paid two pence a week if they had a son. Every time there would be two passenger spaces on a ship, the village had a meeting and put all the lottery numbers in a hat. If it was your number, you're on the way to America! They had to be married to qualify for the lottery. Mother was 15, and Father was 27. They had guts. They never gave up coming to the United States.

He never saw his wife from the time they got aboard until they got off in Boston–and it was 42 days at sea. My mother was domestic help for the high-class passengers. They used my father as part of the crew. He was on a bellows pump–four hours on, four hours off–day and night. They used the ship for cargo, and it didn't come directly to the United States. It must have been a hell of a trip.

They had their own personal utensils and old mattress and before they got into the United States, all that was thrown overboard–out to sea. Tin plates, tin cups, whatever you had. They wouldn't let you come in with a damn thing. That's how rugged it was. That's tough, see, but they did it.

They went to a town called Methuen, Massachusetts, about 25 miles north from Boston.

My father got a job at Beaches' Soap Factory as a fireman shoveling coal and taking care of old man Beaches' pigeons on the roof. They made what they called Worldwide soap. Boy, if you got a bath in that you wouldn't need another one for six months. It was full of lye. He got a dollar a day for 12 hours and a bar of soap, and he walked two miles each way to work.

The old man was a shrewd businessman. He never went to school a day in his life, never. He couldn't either read or write, but smart as a whip. He became a policeman for Methuen and bought a hundred acres with a little old shack on it with just two rooms, and no bath, of course, and a stable for a horse. He bought that on the corner of Mystic and Webb Street. It was right near what they call Mystic Pond. And the translation for Mystic in Indian language is "mistake," and the mistake was made by the runners. People bought land up there years ago with Indian runners [surveyors]. The more you paid the chief, the faster runner you'd get to run around the outskirts of the property. The runner, instead of running around the site, ran all around the damn pond.

A Rough Childhood

I was born at 32 Webb Street, Methuen, MA, the most God-forsaken place you ever saw in your life. All they had for heat was just a kitchen stove and a flat-top range. You run it with wood or coal or whatever you get to put in it. There was no insulation or nothing. Thirty below was common in winter time, very common.

We harvested ice on Mystic Pond for what they called the Lawrence Ice Company. Peter Hawk owned the business. He was one of these huge men that wore a great big fur coat and a big fur hat, a big shot, see. He had me, and another fellow by the name of Bob Gaffney, on a cutter–a plough. They'd measure the ice, they had caulkers, fellows with flat-edge bars that if the water started coming

32 Webb Street

through in different areas, they'd caulk them, so the water wouldn't go through all the crevices and freeze again.

I was on the plough. I was a pretty heavy kid. I wasn't more than fifteen years old. Bob Gaffney was driving the team. This plough–on a farm you raised the handles; on ice, you pushed the handles down so that there was just the heel of the plough that's cutting. I don't know whether I got tired or whether the plough hit what they call a caulker, but the horses stampeded, and the whole bloody thing went through the lake–a team of horses, Bob Gaffney, and me. Well, the horses those days were eight or nine hundred dollars a team and men were fifty cents an hour, so you know what they got out first, don't you? They got the damn horses out.

It was night, you did the cutting for the day crew to get it in. They had a fellow there that had what looked like a wooden drag with a lot of spikes in it, so that he could run with a fast horse. When the horse stopped, this thing would stop because the spikes would stop in the ice. On that he had ropes and tongues that's used in wagons, stuff like that.

So they all went to the one spot to get the horses out. Well, they got the horses out and they got Bob out all right, and they got me out. They took us to the barn where they kept the horses. They put me on the floor in the barn with one of those pot-belly stoves with a blanket over me.

They thought I was dead–they put the blanket right over me. I figured from the smell of the blankets and everything that it was time for me to get some air so I managed to move them around. They were taking better care of the horses than they did with the men, rubbing them down with bags. I got up and walked home. It was about a mile and a half.

My mother raised hell with them, but it didn't do any good. That's the way it went. It was a tough country in those days.

Life as an Apprentice

I quit school;
I just wanted to paint.

Bob Webb, 8 years old (1906)

There was an old man with whiskers in a vacant shop, and I would go down there and watch him through the window. His name was Carl Melby. He used to tell the craziest stories you ever heard in your life. He was a good painter. I got fascinated with him and from there on, that was it. I was down there all the time. The townspeople was after my mother about my not going to school. I'd look through the window at him until my nose would freeze to the glass. After a while, he'd get me to come in and sit down and watch him paint. He was just a talented bum, but everybody fed him. The baker lived close to the vacant shop and he'd get scraps. He was a good-looking man and spoke several languages, French and German. I got so Carl was my buddy. I was about 12. He told me his father was admiral of the Eskimo Navy–which there was no such thing, but I believed him!

Anyway, I quit school. I just wanted to paint. My mother used to get complaints from the people in town. They complained to Mother about me spending so much time with Carl. Carl was a fine man and he loved cats. He had one called Miss Meow, and Miss Meow would do anything he said. She'd get up on his shoulder and crawl around his neck.

What disturbed my old man was Carl used to paint a lot of stuff in barrooms on the walls. I'd hold the step ladder. One picture he painted I'll never forget as long as I live. It shocked me. I was only a kid. It was a picture of a woman lying on a couch with nothing on, with a great big bust stuck up there. Right over the bar. The bartender had some kind of thing on the floor that would pump air. The little tube went over the floor and up in back of the picture. These heavy drinkers would come in there and one would say, "I'd better get off it and get home." And this thing would swell up.

"Oh, my God, I've got to get home." The bartender would say, "Have another." "No, I've got to get home." So he'd let the air out for the next old sucker. I decided to have some fun with it ,so I stuck a hole in the tube and the next time the bartender pumped air he said, "What the hell is the matter with this thing?"

Old Carl started me. He taught me how to mix colors. He'd fall asleep, and I used to grind his colors with linseed oil in a mortar and pestle and put them into pots. The women folks in town didn't think it was right for a kid like me not going to school, but they had no compulsory school in those days, and, of course, there was nothing they could do about it.

I was about fifteen and somebody talked me into going to Salem to see a man who wanted to buy oil paintings. I saw the ad in the Boston paper: Paintings Wanted. I took some down there to see the man. I had 25 cents. The fare was 40 cents to where I was going, something like that. He said, "Boy, I know where you belong. You need a lot of training. I recommend you go see Lamb in Stoughton." He called up Mr. Lamb– F. M. Lamb in Stoughton, Massachusetts–and he told Mr. Lamb, "There's a boy here that you should have."

Fred Mortimer Lamb

For a while, my father studied under Fred Mortimer Lamb, an internationally known artist and muralist. He signed his work, F. M. Lamb. He was born in Middleboro, Massachusetts, in 1861. His studio and home was in Stoughton, Massachusetts. He had studied in London and at the Julian Academy in Paris, where he met a fellow student, John Singer Sargent. Lamb began his career painting animals, then ventured into landscape, still-life, portraits and murals, all in various media.

Lamb taught in the public school system. Students with exceptional talent had private lessons in Lamb's studio and on his field trips. He was a believer in passing on his knowledge and gifts to younger generations. In a booklet he authored entitled, "The Answer," he wrote, "By handing on to our younger men and women what we have learned, we make it nearer possible for them to take up Art where we must drop it, thus laying the foundation for a greater school of American Art."

Lamb became an important part of Dad's life. He eventually lived with the Lambs and became the son they never had. As an adult, Dad's family became their family. Our family traveled from our home in New Jersey to visit Mr. and Mrs. Lamb many times. On one visit, Mr. Lamb painted a portrait of my sister Hannah and me. He duplicated it so each of us would have one. Perhaps the reason I always hated it was because Hannah was wearing the beautiful red coat–the one with the white fake fur collar. I still have the portrait–hidden behind the sofa. Dad recalled his time with Mr. Lamb...

So I went there to study with Mr. Lamb, to paint, every day. He was a great painter. God, he was a great painter. He thought the world of me. My mother gave me some money. In fact, she went with me and talked to Mr. Lamb. She said, "You go your way, lad, and don't pay any attention to anybody but Mr. Lamb." She found me a place to stay in an attic in a house. The woman ran a boarding house and I worked for her running the boarding house to pay my way, cleaning house and all that mess.

Twenty dollars a month was what I had to pay him. I had to earn that twenty dollars a month and seven dollars a week for room and board. A dollar a day was top price in those days for a boarding house in town. I had to earn it nights, later on in the afternoons, Saturday and Sunday. I learned a lot from Lamb. I worked with him on the drop curtains for the Boston Conservatory and other theater drops he was painting.

Mr. Lamb got me acquainted with an old fellow by the name of Ned Nixon who did flagpoles and church steeples all over the place. I used to paint flagpoles and steeples. We had to paint all the flagpoles in the schoolyards. He showed me how to climb a flag pole with two pieces of rope about four-foot long. Then he'd put the paint pot on a hook and hook it over the rope. "I'll get it up there when you get up there. Do as I tell you and you'll be safe." He put the paint pot on the pole rope and pulled it up to me. "Take your time, Rob, I'll let it down as you work down." I got a dollar for that. I got so I didn't know if I was going up or down. The flagpoles were wood. I'd go up and down poles fifty or sixty feet high just like a monkey. I painted every damn flagpole in the county.

He told me this story about when he was a kid. He said he was painting a steeple for a Baptist church, a great, white church. That was when painters wore overalls with straps that crossed on the back. He said the church had a big clock. Sliding down, he got the hour-hand caught on his clothes in the back. People in town started gathering and pointing. The fire department had no ladder that could reach him. He said he looked down the road, and first thing he knew there were horses and wagon loads of hay coming. All the hay was piled up in front of the church steps, and he hung there until six o'clock, then he slid right off into the pile of hay. Crazy as hell. And he said the next morning they expected him to go back and finish painting the steeple.

Mr. Lamb had a recipe for a composition of what to stick canvas on a wall, and so I said, "Mr. Lamb, will you tell me what that is?"

"I will, if you saw up that cord of wood in my yard. It's for the studio. You start the fire in the mornings so I won't have to get up so early. You start the fire each morning and keep it going all day."

The canvas on boards they called double-L Pepperell, they were sheets of canvas that came by the yard. We'd cut them up and put them on boards. He sat in a chair and layered this cloth using a whisk broom and the composition he had in a bowl between each sheet. Then he'd stack bricks on top and lay it down. When it was dry, it would come out flat. I wanted to know the material he had in the basin. So I said, "Mr. Lamb, I lived up to our agreement, will you tell me what it is?"

"I will. You'll learn the same way I did. You just take a big basin and put in two tablespoons of cornstarch and add boiling water to it and stir. That's all. You'll never forget it as long as you live."

I was happy as a lark because I knew how to do it. I've had many people ask me how to do it and I'd always say, if I had a cord of wood, I'd ask you to cut up the wood and keep the fire going for a week. Then I'd tell you.

After I worked for Lamb for a time, he said, "I'm going to give you a chance to learn something fast, Bobby. I'm going to get in touch with John Singer Sargent and ask him if he can use you."

John Singer Sargent

Mr. Lamb loaned me to John Singer Sargent, an internationally known artist who studied with Lamb in Paris years earlier. Sargent came to the United States in 1915 to install the last of a series of murals on Judaism and Christianity at the Boston Public Library. Of course, there was a lot of criticism about them hiring him to come over to do the Boston Public Library. He was American but lived in England. There were so many fine painters around Boston, a city of art–music and art–always has been.

He didn't paint the paintings here, see, it would take too long. He may have been working on them three or four years before he came over. So when he came to Boston he contacted Mr. Lamb and let him know that he was in Boston. Mr. Lamb said, "I've got the guy you want." So I went down there to work with Mr. Sargent.

Sargent was a fine, English gentleman–tall and dignified, with a reddish beard. He was very polite, he never drank or swore on the job. He wore a bowler, and he stuck the handles of his paint brushes in the hat band while he worked. When he wanted one he knew where it was.

It required a lot of paint colors to match them up after the murals were on the walls, and then some changes were made. I made all the colors for him. I used a mortar and pestle and mixed the colors in flower-pot saucers, each one numbered. Sargent worked high up on a scaffold wearing soft, slipper-type shoes and a vest. He'd run the brush up and down his vest to clean it. The vest could stand up by itself. Then he would call out a new number and I would hand it up to him.

He was what you called a dry smoker. He'd cut a cigar in half, light it in the morning and you'd see just two or three puffs of smoke come out. He'd still have it in his mouth at the end of the day, all chewed up with juice running down his chin.

He didn't pay me anything, but he gave me a painting of dancing women. On the back of the painting there's a scrawled inscription, "To Robert Webb," but no signature on the front. Sargent always said there was no need for signatures–only bankers and men in business like signatures.

He wanted me to go back to England with him. He went to see my mother. I think I was sixteen or seventeen years old. She said, "No, I'm not going to let my boy go over there because it won't be long before the United States is in war with England and Germany."

She was right. And, of course, my parents had left England for a better life in the United States.

God, could he paint. He could paint, alright, but he didn't give me a damn cent. I stuck drop cloths under the stairway in the library. That's where I slept. He'd go out for lunch. I'd see other men working there, and I got out of the way. They noticed I had nothing to eat, and they'd give me something.

Life in the Navy

Keep your mouth shut,
make up your mind
what you're going to do,
and do it.

Sailor Bob, 1919

I said, "Christ, the service can't be any worse than this!" I was twenty-one. I tried to get into the Marines first, but when I went to enlist the officer said, "You're not heavy enough." I had seven cents, so I bought seven-cents worth of bananas–five bananas–and I ate them and went back to the Marines, but I couldn't get in. I was two-and-a-half pounds short. I said, "To hell with you. I'll join the Navy." So in February of 1919, they took me in the Navy in Boston.*

I was shipped out of Boston to Norfolk with 600 sailors. They put us on a train to Norfolk. Before we got there, the conductor went through the car and told us the train was going to stop. He said, "We got a flat." What the hell is a flat on a train? I didn't know. I know now. It was a wheel that hadn't been greased, and it wore down flat. Bumpity, bumpity, bumpity, bump. So they had to stop the train. Where do you suppose we were? Williamsburg! The conductor said, "We're going to be here about two hours. Get off. I'll blow the whistle when it's time for you to head back to the train. The second whistle means in five minutes the train is moving. If you ain't on it, goodbye."

So we walked around town. You should've seen Williamsburg. There was nothing there! William and Mary was there. Two-wheel wagons and ducks on the lawn of the old court house, that was there. I liked the oxen.

In Norfolk, I nearly died down there. They had no quarters or nothing. Nothing. I slept on the floor in a peanut warehouse with lots more men. I got sick on peanuts.

Anyway, Sargent and Mr. Lamb had written the commanding officer of the Fifth Naval District. The first thing I know after we got to Norfolk I was grabbed out of line and taken to an office downtown, and that's where Bushnell was–my commanding officer. He was in charge of all the camouflaging for the Navy. He was also Chief of Naval Intelligence. A very fine man.

This camouflaging was just beginning. France had started to camouflage and then the rest of the countries picked it up. They put me on a ship that they had confiscated from the Dutch government that was loaded with copper bolts. I was made chief petty officer, and the man that put me aboard ship with these other three fellows said, "You're not to allow anybody to leave ship and nobody is to come on board. No parcels or mail are to leave, and no parcels or mail are to come on board." He gave each one of us a rifle and said, "You're chief petty officer." Well, I didn't know what that meant. He said, "You're the boss of the other three."

About two days afterwards, a Coast Guard ship came alongside our ship. We were about forty miles outside of Hampton, Virginia The officer put his foot over the rail. I told him, "You're not allowed on board." He said, "I'm from the Office of Naval Intelligence."

I said, "I don't care where you're from, I've got orders to shoot." And he put the other foot over and I said, "I'll shoot you dead. That's my orders." So he went and came back with my commanding officer. My CO said, "Come on with me, Webb." So I went ashore with him. He gave me some money to go to a Naval YMCA to stay there for a couple or three days. He'd already received a message from Sargent about what a colorist I was, recommending me for camouflaging.

They gave me an office in town. Can you imagine that? And another guy–I can't think of his name–his father was senator of North Carolina. He was my helper. They gave us a woodworking shop. They turned over a yacht and a cameraman to us. The yacht was given to the Fifth Naval District by Silvanus Stokes, who was a big hotel owner. He gave it to the Navy provided they'd give his son a job aboard the yacht to keep him out of the combat zone. He and I became close buddies.

I met Rosa in the Navy's photo department where she worked in Norfolk as a yeomanette, the first service rating created for women–most beautiful girl I'd ever seen. Rosa had a job filing photographs for the government. My buddy and I used to take photographs of the ships that were not camouflaged. We took the film in there to be developed. I was first officer, so I used to take film there for my commanding officer, Bushnell. Rosa would check them out for me, and then I'd take the pictures back to him. Then the film was destroyed–[security]. Using the photos as a guide, we'd cut a silhouette out of masonite. It was a different type of wood, similar to plywood. I'd make the designs on the sides of the ships, and these other guys would color them in.

We got orders from Rear Admiral Sims that no ship was to leave port unless it was camouflaged. So I became big overnight, you know. At least I thought I was. We used to make colors by the barrel. I went aboard submarines. I went everywhere. I had a pass, a Naval Intelligence pass, when I was only twenty-one, and I'd go anywhere I wanted to. I'd go on submarines that were in port and ask them to show me the periscopes. When you look through the periscope, it didn't make any difference where *the ship was, it's still just a silhouette. An object on the water is just an object, it wouldn't make any difference how far away it is due to the horizon and the water, see. In the periscope there were two–what looked like hairs, but they weren't hairs. It was spider web. At that time, it was the strongest fiber known, stronger than silk, and when the sub floated, it was always level.*

So I studied that, and I thought they had to get a bead on it, up and down and this way. You couldn't get rid of the ship, don't make any difference what color you painted it, it would still be an object. So I figured the only thing to do with them buggers is to fool them. So I'd paint a submarine on the side of the ship, and I'd write all kinds of cross lines, circles, everything, so they couldn't get a line on it. The front of the ship, I'd paint a bow on it. I'd paint another bow, so when they come up she'd be going the other way. It was interesting as hell.

Then old Rear Admiral Sims wrote my commanding officer, Lieutenant Bushnell. He told him the safety of the ships that leave Hampton Roads are forty percent safe. He recommended me for advanced office, see. So, overnight, I got an increase, and I didn't even know it. Of course, the sailors' pay was only thirty-seven dollars a month. They took thirty dollars of that for insurance for your mother. So that left you seven dollars a month. You couldn't go wrong on seven dollars a month.

Dad's Discharge

Dad's discharge from the Navy uncovered some startling facts. In February, 1918 in Boston's icy weather, Bob enrolled in the Navy for a four-year stint. In 1918, a young man enrolled rather than enlisted. At age 22, he met–and soon married–Rosa Newbern, a young yeomanette. They were married on May 7, 1919, in Elizabeth City, North Carolina. Five weeks after the marriage, Bob returned to Boston with his bride, where he was assigned to the Naval Reserve. His service was cut short, and on September 30, 1921, he was given an honorable discharge. He often said, "The government ran out of money."

Dad's love for his country and his pride over the years he served in the Navy were undisputed. Bob often said, "When I was in the Navy, the ships were made of wood and the men were made of iron. Now, by God, the ships are made of iron and men are made of wood."

While in the Navy, Dad painted a poster encouraging people to buy a bond. The poster features a patriotic young sailor in uniform. It was used by the government in its campaign to raise money.

Dad's discharge document, dated September 30, 1921, reads:

> Robert James Webb, Jr., a Painter 1c (Provisional) #163-23-34 has been discharged from the U.S.S. Headquarters First Naval District and the U.S. Naval Reserve Force, Class 4GS, by reason of ORDER OF SECRETARY OF THE NAVY OWING TO LACK OF FUNDS—ALNAV 67.

Dad, having served 16 months in active service and 27 months in reserve, was just five months short of a full, four-year term. On the back of his discharge papers was the rating:

> Proficiency: Very Good. Sobriety: Excellent. Obedience: Excellent. Percentage of time on sick list during enrollment: Zero.

Dad carried a naval record that entitled him to brag about being one of the iron men on a wooden ship!

The year Dad was discharged, Rosa, his southern beauty who had adjusted to Yankeeland, presented him with their first child, Hannah Louise. She was born April 23, 1921, and named for her paternal grandmother, a midwife, who, no doubt, helped deliver the baby at the home on Webb Street in Methuen, Massachusetts.

While in the Naval Reserve, Dad returned to his love of painting. Here are excerpts from the Lawrence Telegram, a periodical dated February 18, 1922, on his first show:

> Mr. Webb is an artist of great promise and at this exhibition which is the first ever held in Methuen, he is showing a number of his own pictures which have been exhibited at the Pennsylvania Academy of Fine Arts and at the New York Water Club. Besides those, there are several by F. M. Lamb, probably the foremost American painter of the present day, with whom Mr. Webb studied several years.
>
> All of Webb's pictures are taken from nature and the young artist and his master, Mr. Lamb, have spent many hours in the great outdoors reproducing nature as they find it rather than as they think it ought to look.
>
> Mr. Webb studied by himself until he was 16 years old and then he went to Stoughton where for three years he worked with Mr. Lamb, and according to folks who know him, Mr. Lamb became very fond of his ambitious young pupil and took special interest in his progress.

Persistence Rewarded

Keep your mouth shut, make up your mind what you're going to do, and do it.

That's exactly what Bob did, and he was rewarded. The following excerpt is taken from the Virginia Gazette, April 12, 1986, Williamsburg, Virginia:

World War I Vet Finally Gets His Medal

It is only a small bronze button, barely larger than a dime. In the center is a five-pointed star surrounded by a wreath, and the initials *U.S.* The only people entitled to receive them are Army, Navy, and Marine veterans of World War I and their families.

The tiny pin is the lapel button for the W.W. I Victory Medal.

Robert J. Webb, who lives on Neck O'Land Road, knew he had one coming to him, but it took him 64 years to get it. His button finally arrived in the mail last week, after years of letters to the government.

"I sure as hell worked for it, and lots more did too, but I don't give up."

The 88-year-old Webb, a Navy veteran, said his determination was inspired by the example of his former commanding officer, Cmdr. Nathan Bushnell. "Bushnell always said, 'Keep your mouth shut, make up your mind what you're going to do, and do it.'"

Webb, originally from Methuen, Mass., enlisted in the Navy in 1918 and was posted in Norfolk, where his job was to camouflage ships. The work came naturally to him. As a young man, he was color maker for famed painter, John Singer Sargent.

In those simpler times before radar and sonar, ships could be disguised to confuse enemy submarines by having designs painted on them.

"Typical designs were angles and circles. I even painted a submarine on the side of one ship. Colors made no difference as long as they were strong, like dark blue, black, or yellow. We made the craziest ships you ever saw in your life."

He, like thousands of other men, was discharged in 1921 when the armed services ran out of money.

He had sought the button for years. "I wrote to everybody, even the President, and they all passed the buck. They said they didn't make them any more."

His most recent letter was sent to the National Personnel Records Center in St. Louis. The button came from the Defense Personnel Support Center in Philadelphia.

World War II Effort

When the U.S. became involved in W.W. II, Dad had several dozen plywood silhouettes of ships cut and proceeded to paint camouflage designs on them. This was to be his contribution to the war effort.

When he learned about radar and sonar, he said in disgust, "The Navy used to have iron men and wooden ships, now they have wooden men and iron ships." His wooden ships became kindling.

Life at Cà d' Zan

Mrs. Ringling was especially kind
and took an interest
in the workers...
Mr. Ringling was rough but kind.

The Webbs at the Ringling's Estate

In the early 1920s Dad's parents migrated to Lake Worth, Florida, in search of a new life and warmer winters. One by one their children followed, along with their spouses and children. Jane, the oldest, opened her home to the elderly–an acceptable way for a woman to earn a living in those years–and this endeavor evolved into the Eason Nursing Home. After their mother died of breast cancer, Jane cared for Dad's father in this home until he died at the age of 89.

Later the Eason Nursing Home was owned and operated by Jane's daughter, Marian, and her husband. It was passed on to Marian's two sons, Cliff and Ernest Ripley, who eventually sold it. Today the Eason Nursing Home remains one of Florida's largest and most respected nursing homes.

Dad's brother Walter, his wife Ada, and their five daughters followed the family to Florida. Walter, a mason, built an impressive casino and swimming pool in Lake Worth. The casino has been renovated but the Webb influence remains. Walter died young, leaving his wife, Ada, with five young daughters to raise by herself. There were no government assistance programs in those days, so the widow worked at any available job to support her family.

Arthur, the youngest brother, a master auto mechanic, migrated to Florida, built a bungalow, and opened a garage next to Dad's parents on Dixie Highway in Lake Worth. He and his wife Lucy raised three sons. At the onset of World War II, Arthur and his three sons joined the U.S. Coast Guard on the same day. After the war, Arthur taught auto mechanics at a vocational school and invested in the stock market. He became wealthy.

John, the oldest brother, was the only Webb not to migrate to Florida. He had been disabled in World War I and spent most of his life in Veterans' hospitals. As a child, I wrote him letters, and he responded with notes and red, crepe-paper poppies made by hospitalized veterans in recognition of Armistice Day. Although I never met him, I felt close to my only pen pal. One day Dad approached me:

Thelma, Uncle John was a very sick man. He died and left you what he had. You know Aunt Ada's girls don't have a father to take care of them, so I gave those girls what Uncle John left you. That's the best thing to do.

Feeling lucky to have a father, I accepted this and neither the subject nor the amount of the inheritance was mentioned again. At age 8, this was my first lesson in giving to those less fortunate.

Dad was the last to leave Methuen, and in 1924 he drove to Florida with Mom, Hannah, and me–the newest member of the family, a 12-month-old bundle.

The Ringling Mansion

Once in Florida, Dad soon joined with Addison Mizner, a famous architect, who was building mansions for the wealthy in Palm Beach. Mizner kept Dad busy decorating until Dwight James Baum, the architect for John Ringling's home in Sarasota, traveled to see Dad's work. He liked what he saw and borrowed Dad from Mizner to work on Ringling's mansion, Cà d' Zan, which means House of John in the Venetian dialect.

Cà d' Zan: New West Facade
Photo by Giovanni Lunardi

The early years at Ringling's held mixed times for the young decorator, Bob Webb, his beautiful, auburn-haired wife, Rosa, and their young daughters, Hannah and me. In the 1920s, Florida–not yet developed–was a jungle with old country roads meandering along swamps thick with stagnant water, ideal breeding places for mosquitoes. Mom became a victim of encephalitis caused by a mosquito bite she received during an epidemic. This initial illness developed into Parkinson's disease, which was to have a huge effect on Mom, and, secondarily, on her family. Yet I cannot recall a word of complaint or pity from either of my parents concerning this affliction as Mom's health worsened gradually over the years.

In 1971 I approached my father, "Dad, I would like some information about when we lived on Ringling's estate. I remember the story about Mr. Ringling giving Hannah and me dolls for Christmas. Hannah's doll had real hair, and my doll had only an imprint of hair. Childishly, I took scissors and cut the hair off Hannah's doll."

Dad replied...

No, Mrs. Ringling gave you the doll. She was a wonderful lady. She also sent a wagonload of sand for you kids to play in. I went out there one day and there was a rattler sitting on top of that sand pile–as big as your leg. I got a hoe and cut it in half, and you kids went right on playing in the sand. I told her about it, and she sent the gardener down and put mesh wire around the sand pile and added a gate.

We lived in a garage. It was built for Mr. Ringling's Rolls Royce and Mable Ringling's Pierce Arrow. They took the cars out to make a place for me to live. There was a toilet and a sink. That's all. Ringling said, "We'll do that, Mr. Webb, because we have to have you here."

You were about two-years old. Mrs. Ringling asked me if you children had enough milk. At that time Sarasota was considered a long way off, and I had to tell her I hadn't had a chance to go to town. The next day there was a Jersey cow tethered outside our house.

Mr. and Mrs. Ringling were both fine people. Mrs. Ringling was especially kind and took interest in the workers. She loved roses and dressed colorfully. Mr. Ringling was rough but kind. He would get mad and go stomping off, but a few minutes later he would be back, just standing around. He never apologized. He reminded me of a big kid with a big heart.

While I was working there, I bought the first car I ever owned. It was a brand new Dodge and it cost me $560. When I was putting on the license tags, Mr. Ringling and Jimmy Walker, the mayor of New York City, walked up. Mr. Ringling asked me what I was doing, and I told him. He said, "There's no need to do that. You're a painter, just paint C.O.R. on the back bumper. That stands for 'Compliments of Ringling.'"

Later we rented a house on Indian Beach Road [now Bay Shore Road].

I then asked Dad how we came to the Ringling estate. He thought a moment before answering.

I was a tramp decorator, one of a number of first-class American and European decorators who traveled from job to job about the country.

After the war, I came down to Florida and worked for Addison Mizner, a great architect who designed and built many fifteenth-century-style mansions in Palm Beach. He hired me. He told me what he wanted and let me alone. Dwight James Baum, the architect who was designing Ringling's home, came over and looked at my work and persuaded Mizner to loan me for work on Cà d' Zan.

Later Baum loaned me back to Mizner to decorate Riverside Baptist Church in Jacksonville. Then Baum borrowed me back to do the First Baptist Church in Montclair, New Jersey, and jobs in New York. Another architect borrowed me to do a job in Alabama. To tell the truth, I never knew who was paying me.

At Cà d' Zan, I was in charge of the decorating and kept company with some of the greatest painters in the country, without a doubt.

Many of the artisans were Europeans who Ringling brought to America for the job. These included Italian women who made plaster frieze work covered with designs of flowers and leaves.

The frieze work, once it was mounted and coated with 23-carat gold leaf, was the most magnificent work I ever saw in my life. It has become a lost art.

Wherever a good job of decorating was, the tramp artists were there. They could smell 'em. I didn't have to hire them. When I got ready to work, they'd go to work like they'd been hired!

The artisans on decorating jobs would sit around at dinner making sketches of each other. They were broken-down painters who had once been art students but realized that the feel was good but the money wasn't there. So they'd become decorators, damn good ones too.

The Guest Bedrooms

The Ringling house was Venetian–a very beautiful building. There again, Mrs. Ringling let me loose. I had no bosses. She made suggestions of what she wanted. When we got to the bedrooms she said, "I want the doors decorated."

I said, "Well, that won't be too bad to do."

"But," she said, "I want the insides of the closet doors decorated, not the outsides."

I thought, well, that's a new one.

"When my guests open the door," she continued, "I want them to have a surprise."

And they were one-panel doors, most of them. So I'd decorate them with birds, and flowers, and all sorts of things. She was very happy about it.

Mable's bedroom hall door was decorated by Keppa Buck, brother of Frank "Bring 'Em Back Alive" Buck. The flower work on her bedroom door panel was very well done, but the artist was quick-tempered. So she didn't interfere with him.

She brought me postcards with bright color designs from her trips. I used them for ideas for her bathroom closet and cabinets, and I surprised her by painting a design on the inside of her medicine cabinet. She was so pleased, I had to do the medicine cabinets in all five guestrooms.

Mabel's Guest Room Closet
Photo by Giovanni Lunardi

The Dining Room

Mrs. Ringling took great interest in the decor of the mansion. She'd plan a trip to Europe and tell me what she was going to buy. I'd plan the decorating around it. She had a great love for cameos and liked to have them adorning the walls and ceilings.

One day Mrs. Ringling brought me a tray of brooches, combs, and unset cameos she had purchased from the Gavet collection and asked to have them included in the decoration. I copied them freehand on the ceiling panels in the dining room. Each design came from her collection. It took me about three months. I'd leave the tray of cameos on the ladder overnight. In those days they were safe.

The plaster ceiling in the state dining room is coffered but appears to be fine wood. It was finished in 23-carat gold. Boiled tobacco juice was used as a glaze to tone down the bright embellishments.

They had lots of guests, politicians, celebrities. I met Jimmy Walker, Florenz Ziegfeld and his wife, Billie Burke, Alfred Smith, the governor of New York, and Will Rogers.

Ringling had a big dinner one night and Will Rogers was there. He asked

Dining Room Ceiling (Detail)
Photo by Terry Shank

Will to entertain the guests, as was his custom. Later Will informed John he owed him $200. John asked, "Why? You were a dinner guest."

Will replied that since his wife had not been invited, he assumed he was there to entertain. And John Ringling paid him!

I spent four years working there. It was a big job. Barges appeared out on the bay from nowhere with marble and other building supplies. There must have been 150 workmen, working all hours. Gnats and mosquitoes were horrible. Workmen wore African hats with netting hanging down to protect their sweating necks and faces. Originally there wasn't much heat in the house. Later they had hot water and hot-air heat.

The old fellows who worked there were real artists. We went to work at any time, day or night, and we would work several days without rest. You don't find that anymore. Some of them were German, some French, and some were brought to this country by Ringling especially for the job. They had a habit of initialing their work. I've found some in several places.

The Vaulted Room

Valuables and liquor were stored in the third-floor vaulted room, adjacent to the game room.

"My Little Doggies"

Ringling, he'd have a barge load of booze come in. Those were Prohibition days. And he used to drink this Black and White Scotch. There were little miniature black and white Scotties tied around the neck of the bottle. So I stored some of his liquor, ...used to have it come in at night. They had no electricity on at the time, so we put lanterns on the steps all the way up to his large vault on the top floor. It had an iron door like a bank vault. I knew the back stairway. I'd sneak up and down the back stairway, and I would hide it out in a lumber pile–several cases of it out there–and come back and bring some more until I got tired of going up and down that narrow stairway.

A couple of weeks after it came in, Ringling went down in the yard where his cars were parked and you kids were playing in a sand pile out there in the front where we lived. He walked over to you, Thelma, and asks, "Are you Mrs. Webb's little girls?" And you say, "Yes."

He asks, "What have you got there?"

You say, "These are my little doggies."

"Where did you get those?"

"'Oh, Daddy gave us a whole lot of them."

"'You tell your Daddy I want to see him."

So I got in the middle of that one. I got hell for stealing his booze. But how would he miss anything like that with a whole barge load? I mean a barge! They'd pick it up at sea. Oh, he had some terrific parties, but I got my share of it. Of course, I was one of the very few that lived on the estate. It was always locked up at night. I made out alright.

The Game Room

The game room has a ceiling with fantasy murals by Willy Pogany depicting John and Mable Ringling parading among costumed revelers in a Pageantry of Venice carnival celebration. There is a humorous caricature of a dancing Willy Pogany dripping paint from his over-sized brush as he dances. Pogany was a costume and set designer for Ziegfeld's Follies and for the 1930s Hollywood films. He was a short, skinny, glass-eyed Bohemian full of talent.

Willy Pogany
Photo by Jay Wright

The Ballroom

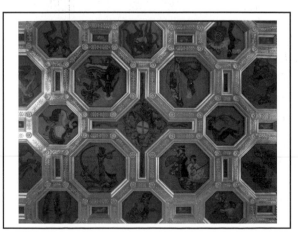

BallroomCeiling (Detail)

Pogany also did the extraordinary ceiling in the ballroom where Dances of Nations are pictured. John and Mable are depicted in the right corner facing the bay. The dancing couples were painted on canvas then set in shadow box frames and I decorated them with 23-carat gold. We used $8,000 worth of gold leaf sheets. Gold leaf lasts indefinitely. Mr. Ringling wanted a glaze over the gold leaf to take the glare away.

Rottenstone and buttermilk were used on the walls. The home was always filled with flowers, and the teakwood floor in the ballroom got plenty of use at Mrs. Ringling's lovely parties.

They had guests by the dozens, and a large party might go on for days–eating, sleeping, swimming, and boating. Pleasure and business were combined.

Corner Designs by Willy Pogany

John's Bathroom

John Ringling was a strong, boastful man who loved being first. He came in when I was marbleizing the toilet in his bathroom to match the bathtub carved out of a solid piece of Siena marble. "Just think, Webb, I'll be the first man in the United States to take a bath in a tub made of solid marble with gold fixtures!" I shot back, "The hell you will. I've been taking a bath in that tub every day for five weeks."

He left in a rage, and I continued to marbleize the toilet. But he never held a grudge. I don't suppose anybody outside of the family or some of the leaders of the circus knew him any better than I did.

John was a big man, and he was just as big in principle as he was in size. He always had a cane and was forever smoking cigars.

John's Bathtub
Photo by Jay Wright

The Great Room

The focal point of the 31-room Ringling home is the immense living room–or court room–rising two and a half stories to a coffered, pecky-cypress ceiling, which frames an inner skylight of six panels of English lac glass in hues of rose, ivory, blue-lavender, and straw. Suspended from the center of the ceiling is a huge crystal chandelier, which originally hung in the old Waldorf-Astoria Hotel in New York City.

This magnificent room is the central space around which all the other rooms are arranged. Decorative and unusual pecky-cypress falsework is suspended from large, steel trusses that run from the room's north and south walls. Huge columns on the first floor are faced with Mexican onyx.

Court Room

Dad continued his verbal tour:

Ringling's had large dinner parties in this room. The fireplace is false. It was an afterthought of Mrs. Ringling. There is no chimney. The panes of glass in the doors that open to the marble terrace facing the bay are Venetian glass. Lots of colors there and in the skylights to soften the bright sunlight.

John and Mable loved organ music. Mrs. Ringling would put a roll in the organ, and the house would be full of music. It could be played manually or electrically. They paid $50,000 to have it custom built. This builder installed the pipe organs on two other jobs I did: the church in Jacksonville and the church in Montclair, New Jersey. We both came from the Boston area. We had good times together.

The main ceiling was made out of pecky cypress. Pecky cypress was used to a great extent in Florida years ago. The cypress trees were underwashed and fell over into the waters...been there for hundreds of years with just a stump sticking up and the roots. Then worms got into it, and there is something about the tree that they liked.

Then somebody got the idea, and they cut them off and brought them in and put them through a mill. It made beautiful wood. Cypress doesn't rot, you see, so these holes and worm movement in the wood became nationally known.

They've used so much of it that it just doesn't exist. There's no more of it, see, but it was beautiful wood. Then we had to decorate that stuff. It wasn't easy over top of all those worm holes and thirty feet up to the ceiling!

The designs I used on the beams I painted from stencils, but I cut the stencils freehand. Both John and Mable loved the colors red, gold, and blue. Mr. Ringling said the colors were too bright, so they were toned down with buttermilk and rottenstone.

The second floor has a balcony on three sides that overlooks the great room. The columns and balustrade are of glazed terra cotta. Mrs. Ringling's bedroom and five guest rooms open onto the balcony. I decorated the ceiling around the balcony, and in the ceiling on the first floor I signed my name and age: R.Webb 27.

Note: To find Dad's signature, step into the great room from the ballroom, turn right, look up toward the corner. The signature is visible within the decoration.

I knew Mr. Ringling was a marvelously creative man, so I asked Dad to tell me more about him.

Well, he died leaving $360 in his checking account. His wealth was tied up in property, but the banks were after that. But he lived like a king while he was living. That's what he wanted to do. He did exactly what he wanted to do. He didn't leave nothing. He wouldn't have left that if he had lived a little longer. He was a big spender.

A fine man. A wonderful man. He was animal crazy. The man was absolutely crazy—he wasn't afraid of no animal. He knew how to handle them. You'd think he was another animal.

I remember old Gargantua, an ape, weighed 640 pounds and had an arm-spread of unbelievable length. A huge animal—huge. They had to feed her with a snow shovel under the space of the cage door. They fed her bananas and all kinds of fruits that they got from Africa. I think she comes from Africa. Yes, African jungles. To tame her, he had a cage built out in front of his house, an iron cage and a bathroom for her made out of straw and bamboo stuff. She was a beautiful animal. And he had the key. He locked it up. He wouldn't let nobody in there. He kept a screen fence around it so nobody would torment her.

But that was a beautiful animal. My God, that animal was human. But, of course, they were afraid of her. Good God, she could take a hand and break you in half. But she died of pneumonia in the circus.

I helped a German man by the name of Bustabaum paint side curtains. He painted all the side curtains: the fat lady, snake charmers—exaggerations of everything—but the people loved it. I worked with him one season, and then I had enough of that.

All this stuff was done at the winter quarters, and then they'd be taken on the traveling show. These side show curtains were the size of cages. They'd have a side-show curtain like this, and then the cages for the animals were inside of that. They'd fold this up like that, and bring it up like this, then on top was where the men slept who took care of the animal. Understand what I mean?

I'd say at least between five- and eight-hundred people were employed. And they were in three different classes, but they all ate in the same tents, same food wherever they eat. Ringling too. He'd walk in and eat his breakfast and lunch same as everybody else did. It was good food—wholesome.

He had a carload of raw meat a day from a packing company to feed the animals. The animals ate just as good as the people because you can't feed animals stale meat, and you can't feed people stale meat. So everybody shared with the animals, the food. So they fed well, but they didn't pay nothing.

The circus was a great outfit. Fantastic people. But, as I say, they had three classes. The professional trapeze artists were mostly German and Italian. They stayed with their own group and they were mostly families and kids. And they were good people; high-class.

The animal trainers were high-class too, absolutely. They had to be, no monkey business. You get in a cage with seven or eight lions, you can't be messing around, you know. You got to know what you're doing. You got to know something. I've seen some pretty close calls, too—pretty close ones. I don't know how the hell they do it because you wouldn't dare go near them. Of course, they carried pistols, but maybe they'd be loaded, maybe they wouldn't. I don't know. I never saw anybody shoot a pistol, but they used whips, chairs.

Tramp Artist: The Life of Robert Webb

I found out afterward there was always one of these chairs that had round legs, something they could put their arm through and hold like that, then I found out afterwards the bottom of the chair was painted bright red. See, that's the only color an animal can see is red. I have an idea they used pokers to begin with–hot pokers–to let them know what red meant. If you know what I mean.

Animal training is not a sissy's job.

Cà d' Zan Changes Hands

John and Mable Ringling's marriage of 25 years was amiable and loving. Mable Ringling died in 1929, having enjoyed only three years at Cà d' Zan. Mable was younger by nine years, and John had not contemplated life without her. He did remarry a wealthy widow, Emily Haag Buck. The marriage was a disaster, and in his will he left her one dollar.

In 1932, John Ringling suffered a blood clot in his right leg. The same year he was ousted as head of The Greatest Show on Earth. Two years later, he sustained a near-fatal heart attack. After John's death in 1936 in New York City, his property was in litigation, and the State of Florida did not obtain full possession of Cà d' Zan until 1946.

Renovations Begin

In 1960, Dad was commissioned by Florida to restore his work in Cà d' Zan. He accomplished this by selecting a project for each winter. This enabled him to have Mom in the warm, Florida sun for the winter season, and in Williamsburg during spring, summer, and fall, when the climate is mild.

Dad purchased a mobile home on De Soto Road, convenient to Ringling's mansion. It was an ideal arrangement. Mom enjoyed the fellowship in the park, and Dad had great satisfaction and fun restoring Cà d' Zan. Before the renovations began, Dad evaluated the condition of Cà d' Zan and remembered Ringling's estate in its day:

There's been normal deterioration, but it's still a fabulous place. It probably cost $1.5 million to build, and houses aren't built like that today. It would cost too much to keep them up. You would need 10 or 12 servants.

Some painters have taken the easy way out and painted over the original work. I'm having to do a lot of archaeological work to find the original colors.

The dock is gone. It was in the rear of the mansion on the bay side and was made of barrels and planks. Mrs. Ringling's gondola was lost in a storm. Barges carrying furniture and materials for the house were unloaded there. During Prohibition, the barges carried liquor to stock Mr. Ringling's private bar. Prohibition didn't mean a thing here. They had a big yacht anchored out in the bay, the Zalophus. *It sank. I don't know where the name came from, but their train was named* Jomar, *after him and Mable. It was beautiful. They had no bunks, it was bedrooms. It had three bedrooms and a bedroom for the Japanese cook they had aboard. Ringling had a personal coach that followed the circus. It was decorated with 23-carat gold! God, it was a beautiful train. They were the days!*

Shortly after the renovations began, I drove to Sarasota to surprise Mom and Dad with a visit. I entered Cà d' Zan and saw Dad standing on a ten-foot scaffold working on the ceiling at the entrance to the formal dining room. Quietly I walked toward him, stood at the base of the scaffold, and said, "Mr. Webb, if you had done a good job the first time, you wouldn't be up there in your old age doing it over."

Without missing a stroke of his brush, he promptly replied, "Young lady, that's the way I planned it!"

On the original decorating of Cà d' Zan, John Ringling and Dad were sometimes in disagreement. The ceiling in Ringling's bedroom was one such contention. Ringling had purchased a large, oval, mythological painting, *Dawn Driving Away the Darkness*, painted in 1735 by Jacob deWit for a house in Haarlem, the Netherlands.

Dad continued his narrative:

We put it up with lead and varnish. It was a hell of a job. When Ringling saw it he said, "Webb, can you do anything with the rest of the ceiling?"

Robert Webb: Renovating, 1960

"Yes, I can carry this painting right out to the corners, all the way around and paint cherubs in the ceiling–the whole works, clouds and everything."

I got it done. A year later Ringling said, "My God, you can't tell the difference."

For years this disturbed Dad. He had wanted to frame the oval painting, and then fill in the corners with a blending color. Smiling with anticipation he said, "Now, I'll have my way, which will last longer than Ringling having his way!"

For several years I begged my father to teach his skills to an apprentice so his art would not become lost. Dad decided that making the oval frame might be a good time to share his knowledge. He drove to William and Mary College in Williamsburg, Virginia, and explained to the art director his willingness to teach a talented student. Soon an eager art major arrived at Webb's Acre for an interview. Dad gave great detail:

I'll teach you how to make an oval frame using plaster of paris. Then we'll go to Sarasota. I'll show you how to clean the painting that's on the ceiling, remove the canvas painting from the outer edges. I'll show you how to put up the frame. Then I'll teach you how to gold leaf.

The young man seemed pleased and asked only one question, "How much will you pay me?"

The interview ended in an explosion that lasted days:

The son-of-a-bitch! I told him what I would teach him, offered to take him to Sarasota to help on the job and his only goddamn question was, "How much are you going to pay me?" I'm supposed to pay the bastard to teach him what it took me a lifetime to learn? No wonder the country is going to hell. I'll do the bloody job by myself!

And he did.

The oval frame of plaster of paris was made in sections in his studio barn in Williamsburg. The sections were wrapped in blankets and carefully packed in the car trunk. He drove to Cà d' Zan and unloaded each section. He removed his canvas from the corners and outer edges of the painting. "I gave them to the city dump, but I should have given them to somebody else since they had all these cherubs and clouds."

The frame sections were secured around the edge of the deWit oval painting, then gold leaf was applied. When the ceiling was completed, Dad lay on the floor beneath the painting, "Damn, that's beautiful! That's the way it should have been thirty-five years ago."

To celebrate his triumph over successfully completing the ceiling, Dad decided to have dinner at a restaurant, "...with a table cloth and a real napkin. I'm not using those damn paper napkins."

Mom, Dad, and I were led to a round table close to another table where several people were seated, laughing and talking about their day's sightseeing in Sarasota. Dad, who was on his sociable level of drink, overheard their conversation and did not hesitate to lean toward them. "Did you visit the Ringling home yet?"

One in the group answered, "No, we haven't. We plan to do that tomorrow."

Dad leaned further into their circle, "Let me tell you a few facts about the home."

Mom, hoping to stop something before it was to be, said, "Bob, you've had too much to drink. You're making a fool of yourself."

"Rosa, I'm just going to tell them a few things." And he leaned further into the group.

"Oh, Bob..."

Knowing the situation was hopeless, I whispered, "Mom, forget it. Just forget it. Let him make a fool of himself. They won't know whether he's telling the truth or not."

Mom and I listened as Dad introduced himself as one of the artists that had decorated the home originally and was now restoring his work. The captive audience was enthralled with his stories...one after another.

Mom waited quietly for whatever was yet to come. I sat in silent prayer hoping that somehow this would end...soon.

Finally, Dad reached into his coat pocket for the small pad and pencil he always carried. He scratched a note and handed it to a woman at the table. "You give this note to the people at Ringling's tomorrow, and they'll let you in as my guest."

The note was graciously accepted, folded, and placed in a pocketbook.

Dad sat up straight and gave his attention to his family. With a smile of satisfaction he said, "I bet that was a surprise for those people!"

Mom's response was a glare that kept him quiet through dinner and dessert.

The Foyer

Dad restored the foyer in 1961. The heavy double walnut doors leading into the front foyer (42" x 24") are from the John Jacob Astor house in New York. The gold painted Solomonic columns came from Venice, Italy, in the 1920s.

Dad said:

Originally, I painted on canvas to be applied between the walnut beams in the ceiling. Ringling came to me and asked me to hurry and finish because he was running out of time

Unfinished Foyer Panel
Photo by Terry Shank

and money. I put my brush down and said, I'm finished. You can look at the panel nearest the doorway to the lounge and see where I stopped.

In restoring the ceiling, Dad retained the beautiful renaissance red background and the scrolled gray leaves and grapes with an antique finish.

There are five arches in the foyer that open to the great room.

Dad refinished the lounge ceiling the same year. He remembered the walls were originally painted pale gray and brushed over with silver, metallic paint.

The portraits of John and Mable Ringling painted by Savely Sorine in 1927 hung in the lounge. Dad always said they were a very good likeness.

The Ballroom

Dad continued his reminiscences about Cà d' Zan:

Restoring the ballroom [1962] was a big job. The twenty-eight paintings–all on canvas by Willy Pogany denoting folk dances of twenty-eight nations–had to be removed, cleaned, and retouched. The plaster on the ceiling had to be repaired. Then the canvas paintings were reapplied to the ceiling. I replaced the 23-carat gold leaf on the interlocking frames of each painting. The gold leaf itself is worth about four thousand.

From a letter Dad sent dated January 6, 1963:

> I am getting the rough work done this trip so I won't have to do so much next fall. I feel much better working. A strong back and a weak head seems to be my make-up.

The next three winters, 1964 through 1966, Dad worked in the Great Room. Excerpts from letters to me tell it all:

> I must have been very daring back then. It's a hell of a long way up there.

> I'm having a time matching the original colors. I don't know where I got some of them. I miss the old fellows who worked here. They were real artists.

Several times during the restoration Dad returned home laughing, "I got a hell of a kick out of a note I found today."

He had discovered a forgotten note written as a young artist, a note he left on a ceiling beam, intended to be found by a future restorer—never dreaming he would be the one!

In one letter he wrote:

> The carpenters built me a good scaffold with a handrail around, strong enough for elephants. They want to keep me in good shape for the future. I have a chair on the scaffold, also drinking water and a pail to put it in.

> George, the man that works with me, is having a ball. He says he'll be glad when I go home. He's doing all the work, and I get the money.

Great Room Ceiling
Photo by Geoffrey Steward

The Bird Cage

In 1968, the curators at the Ringling Museum led Dad into the museum basement. They showed him boxes with large pieces of broken delft and asked if he knew what it was.

Yes, that was Mrs. Ringling's cage for her pet parrots, Laura and Jacob. I don't remember the name of the third one. But I did an oil portrait of the three parrots. It was a beautiful cage. I can fix it.

The boxes of broken delft were taken to Cà d' Zan's kitchen and the project for the winter season began.

I was visiting, and Dad said he could use an extra pair of hands with the birdcage. While we worked, he talked about Ringling's original staff:

Sophia was the cook and the boss of the house. There were two housemen, a butler, a personal maid, and two general maids.

Mr. Ringling liked turtle soup, Sophia would get the gardener to find turtles from the bay. The hard tile in the kitchen and pantries were covered by soft tile to keep Sophia happy. She ran this house. All the rooms in the service wing were painted light green because that's what Sophia wanted.

She wanted the two Westinghouse, automatic-electric ranges placed side-by-side with the ovens on either end.

Bird Cage
Photo by Giovanni Lunardi

As Dad and I worked on the cage in the makeshift workshop in the kitchen, a continuous stream of tourists stepped into the roped area and without fail one of them would exclaim, "Oh, look at the Westinghouse automatic stove!"

Dad responded with a raised eyebrow, "This job is good for old age."

It was painstaking surgery, but with the aid of glue and coat hangers, we restored Mrs. Ringling's handsome delft cage.

The birdcage did not occupy all of Dad's time. I received the following letter when I returned home. Dad was trying his skill at gardening in the mobile park.

> I wanted to stick a pipe in the ground to hang my water hose on. On my first dig with the posthole digger, I cut the plastic water line to the entire park. God, I thought I had struck white gold! The manager ran over, "If you read the damn rules, you'd find out you aren't supposed to dig holes."

The pipe was repaired, and I dug three more holes and planted potatoes. They'll have potatoes this summer after I'm gone.

Letter dated: January 20, 1972:

I have done a little work on a mirror and two pieces of furniture. I used the kitchen at the Ringling home for a shop. They are putting in air conditioning all through the house. What a mess. It is not for me.—I just cannot take it anymore, I am not what I used to be.

I don't intend to do much. Work is one thing I have always had plenty of. I just wish I could hand over to one of my grandchildren what I can do. But it takes so long and such small pay. You cannot blame young men not wanting to work for nothing.

If I do say so, my work is fast becoming a lost art or they would not want me at my age.

Letter dated: February 13, 1972

I have not been doing much. I am fed up with work. I plan on starting to paint a few small pictures. Your mother will like that. She tells me I am the town drunk, my clothes are never pressed and I have a big belly and I look like a frog. Nothing like being attractive.

It was 1972–the last year Dad, who was then 75, worked on Cà d' Zan–but it was not his last winter in Sarasota. For several more years Mom enjoyed warm sunshine in their mobile home while Dad lived life full-speed-ahead, free of work obligations for the first time since he was fourteen-years old.

For additional pictures of the Ringling Cà d' Zan mansion, see "Glimpses of Cà d' Zan" on page 193.

Life Ecclesiastic

When I was a boy
an old preacher gave
me a Bible.
He wrote my name
in it
and the date it was
given to me.

Riverside Baptist Church

Dad often mentioned an octagonal church in Jacksonville, Florida, that he had decorated for Addison Mizner, the famous architect who designed the fabulous mansions for the wealthy in Palm Beach during the Roaring 20s.

Dad was working for Mizner in Palm Beach when Dwight James Baum borrowed him for Ringling's Sarasota mansion. In 1974, Dad visited Riverside Baptist church in Jacksonville and shared his recollections with me.

Riverside Baptist Church

Addison Mizner, who was the architect here, borrowed me back from D.J. Baum when I was working at the Ringling mansion. Addison asked him if I could come over here.

I came alone and everywhere I went the same men would be following me. They were mostly German and Italian. They seemed to know where I was all the time. They'd come and go to work without me saying anything about it.

The walls here appear to be blocks but they are hollow, terra-cotta tile. It makes a good, solid wall. Inside and out they were plastered. It's light construction in weight and it's fast handling. You can go up four or five feet a day and go up another four or five feet the next day because there isn't much mortar between the joints.

And what the Italians did, they would check the plaster with their cheeks. They would blow their cheek out and rest it against the plaster, and when they felt it to be a certain temperature, they would know it was time to score the cement to give the effect of block.

If you get close to inspect, I think you'll find the marks of what they call a walk rack. It's a tool that's used in sidewalks a great deal. And that's what they did the block pattern with.

It was suggested Dad could put to rest the one rumor about the tiles on the roof. The story was that a woman whose thigh was just the right proportion was used for a cast. All tiles came from that cast. Dad laughed and continued his story.

That's the truth. In Spain right now, you go through the countryside and you'll find a big opening in a field of clay, and they dig the clay up and put it into vats in the ground, and they have kids after school with no shoes on stomping in this clay so they can use it. It might be this roof here represented one family and they made it on their legs. The women would put the clay over their legs and cut it with a cord. They'd use their legs for a cast. Then a kid would come and take them and put them out in the field and let the sun dry them out. If you get them all the same size, as you have here mostly, they must have come from the same family. These families were very proud of what they did. Buyers would go from one place to another and make sure they were all the same size.

At one time, the whole floor of the sanctuary was the same as the tile that runs up the aisle. I'm sure it was. I believe it's underneath the asphalt tile. The reason I think they put the asphalt where the benches are...this tile here when it's wet is very dangerous, especially with wax on it. It had a variation of the colors, the same as the tile on the roof.

Heraldry and Such

Thirteen colorful shields adorn the front of the church balcony.

They're coats of arms. It was a habit years ago that a family coat of arms would be used in the church, especially if they were great donators to the church. It could be plaster, ceramic, or a painter's insignia. I designed and painted these, but I don't remember the purpose of them. I rubbed umber and buttermilk on them to tone down the color.

On each side of the entrance door is a gargoyle of a scapegoat head. The myth is that evil spirits could not pass between goat's heads. If you were a bad person or had problems, the evil that was with you would stop at the door.

The goats' heads were cast here. Other pieces were made here, too. A nun's head and a bird. That's where the trouble started. I always said a good Baptist church had two sides-one for, and one against. But see, these men [workmen], some of them were Catholic. The German people and the Italian people were naturally Catholic, and they can't do anything without leaving some feeling of the Catholic Church. That's what they did, and right away there was some objections by the congregation. It's difficult to get a group of men like that without leaving a feeling of what they were brought up to believe, see, as much as they try to avoid it. It's still in their hearts, and they do leave something. It's a family thing.

All the interior wood is pecky cypress, and we didn't paint it–only with the ornamental decorations. The front door was made here, but the pecky-cypress lumber came from the east coast of Florida. You can't beat it.

The decorations on the beams over the choir and in the main portion of the ceiling are fifteenth-century Renaissance. A great deal of the designing of it came from a palace in Florence, Italy, and I had the plates. I bought them in New York, and I carried the plates with me everywhere. And that's where the decoration came from.

They're in a loose-leaf book, and it has the original colors of what they have there and, of course, the palace is a much larger building than this, much larger. They are paper plates. I used the patterns and stencil paper–two by four feet long, something like that–and cut them out with sharp knives, cut them on a plate of glass.

A lot of the buildings I've done are of the same period of work, but not the same designs you have here. I never use the same designs in two different buildings. So this is the original as far as that goes.

The only colors we used were the primaries, which is red, blue, and yellow, the same as your sunset and the same as your rainbow. There are 17 secondary colors that you can make from the three primaries. After the 17 secondary colors you get hues of colors. Hues are not used in my work. It's used in fabrics, wallpaper, and all that sort of thing. But I don't go past the 17 secondary colors.

The Church Dome

I asked Dad if he decorated the beams in the dome before they were put up.

No, there would have been no roof. That's the roof structure. It's 30 feet high, resting on eight enormous beams crisscrossing on columns that support the dome. See what I mean? I went up on a ladder and came down on a rope. Oh, boy, it was hot, no air. A plank scaffold shut off all air, you see. Worked up there with just shoes and pants on. That particular ceiling took six weeks.

When I was a boy, an old preacher gave me a Bible. He wrote my name in it and the date it was given to me. It was a very important Bible to me, and I had it in my lug-

gage when I came here. When I finished the stenciling up there, I left it on top of one of those big beams and it's laying up there right now. It's still there.

Church Walls

I asked Dad about the aging of the church walls.

Inside we had to do it by hand. What I mean by that is we had old fire extinguishers and we wet the walls. Then we put some lamp black and burnt umber in a pail of buttermilk and mixed it up. Then we applied it to the damp wall, and it would run down and age the wall.

But outside, I called a fire department man. The fire department came out and wet the walls outside, and we applied the same colors outside around the windows and let it run down, wash down, and we had to follow the shade around to keep it from drying too fast. And that's how the outside was done.

We bought gallons of buttermilk. What we didn't drink, we put on the walls. We aged the inside wood with buttermilk and rottenstone.

Rottenstone is very similar to a dry cement. That's what it is...rottenstone. You pulverize it by putting it through a mill and grinding it down to a powder and that was used after the buttermilk was applied; dusting it on added age to it.

Walking toward one wall, Dad observed:

It's not right. It shouldn't have that black on it. I can't understand why it should be there in the first place if there was a proper job putting in the heat ducts. It's a soot of some sort.

Well, one thing you need to do is change your furnace filters a little more often. How to clean it? I'd have the baker prepare a large amount of bread dough. I'd take that dough and roll it up and down the wall and let the bread dough pull out the soot. If it were my church, I'd leave it alone. It doesn't look that bad.

The main thing is if you start trying to do something in an area like that, you're gonna spoil what you have in other places.

From my life's experience, if you want something done as technical as that and you know how it's done, get somebody who don't know nothing, and have them do just exactly as you tell them. If you get somebody that thinks he knows...goodbye job...that's that.

If I were you, I'd leave it alone.

Remembering Addison Mizner

Mizner never gave me directions. He just simply said, "Here's the job," and he didn't bother me no more. Of course, I worked with him before in Palm Beach on those big mansions.

When I was working for him in Palm Beach, there was nothing unusual about him coming on a job with just his pajamas on and a pair of slippers and a monkey on a cord. And the monkey would jump off his shoulder, up on some chandelier, and start fooling around, and people would come to get him out. Mizner just paid no attention to them at all. He was a very fine man. He was a big man, and he had three brothers. They're all big boys. I knew two of them. One was sheriff of Palm Beach County and controlled the legal operations. Another was a bootlegger and controlled all the illegal whiskey. They made a fortune. Another brother was a preacher. God knows they needed a preacher.

Mizner wasn't any denomination, but he promised his mother, a devout woman, he would design a church in her memory. He charged no fee for the design or for over-seeing the construction, and it was the only church he designed.

Recollections

The church was built when I came here. I just came to do the decorating on the walls and ceilings and the antiquing of it, inside and out. I worked here at least eight or nine months. I know it was summertime when I came, then winter, then summertime again.

I'm very happy to be back to look at the building. It's the first time I've been back since I did it. I think it was 52 years ago, and I guess they thought I was dead.

River Road Baptist Church

Dad accepted many side jobs while employed at Colonial Williamsburg. In 1955, the River Road Baptist Church in Richmond, Virginia, commissioned Dad to do the ecclesiastical coat of arms above the door of the chapel. The coat of arms was adapted from similar ones found on buildings in Colonial Williamsburg.

My family and I were active members, and Dad's grandkids had fun bragging about the man on the scaffold being their grandfather.

The following is an excerpt describing the symbolic meaning of the coat of arms from the pastor's page by Dr. Vernon Britt Richardson:

In the center is a Maltese cross on a field of cobalt blue. This is surrounded by a golden ring suggestive of eternity. This center is flanked by two golden griffins, mythological figures half-lion and half-eagle to symbolize that man is an earthly and spiritual being. Laying on top of the circle is an open Bible on which is printed a portion of John 14. Around the circular medallion is a decorative design made of thistles–to symbolize the hardships Christians must face–the bursting pomegranate for regeneration or the new birth, a blooming rose for the beauty of godly lite, and the laurel for victory. The entire composition is topped by a lamp of gold–the light of the world–and is based upon a streamer bearing the Latin words, pax et lux (peace and light).

How fitting it is for us to bring to mind the symbol set forth in the crest over the door of our first building. The beauty presented is the beauty of holiness and discipleship, for the symbols include a cross, thistles, and a laurel wreath, a traditional sign of victory presented only after the hard race is won.

Religious Murals

Previously in the early 1930s, Dad and his mentor, F.M. Lamb, painted five murals in Lamb's studio in Stoughton, Massachusetts. Four are in the chapel of the First Baptist Church in Montclair, New Jersey (now Christ Church). In 1944, the fifth mural titled, *Suffer The Little Children To Come Unto Me* found a home in the Bellamy United Methodist Church in Gloucester, Virginia.

I traveled to Gloucester in 1996 to see the mural. I was expecting a little, white country church tucked in the woods. It was a surprise to find a large, beautiful, brick church with over 800 members.

I was early for the Sunday service, and as I walked through the front entrance I felt Dad peering over my shoulder, "So you finally came to see? It took you long enough!"

I smiled a silent response, "Yeah, Dad, I finally came to see."

Not only did I feel Dad's presence, but the congregation happened to sing Mom's favorite hymn, *The Old Rugged Cross.* I had warm feelings of being home in this church–a church I had never seen before.

I met an 87-year-old lady who remembered when Dad was installing the mural. "I loaned Mr. Webb my sheets to hang over the mural when he finished his days work. He didn't want anyone to see it until it was completed. He painted it in about three weeks."

Never could an artist paint a mural of this magnitude in three weeks! Actually, it is two murals, painted on canvas and joined in the center. The three weeks was for installing and extending the two ends of the canvas and for touch up. In the top center, to the right of Christ's head, is a seam where the two canvases join.

After the congregation left the sanctuary, I walked toward the front and sat on the steps leading to the minister's pulpit. From there I could view the 8 x 24-foot mural that covers the full length of the wall over the entrance doors. I had the overwhelming feeling of being one of the little children walking toward Jesus.

This is the mural that hung on the garage wall when I was a child in Cedar Grove, and each time Dad drove in or out of the garage we would pass Jesus. To me, it was just something hanging on the garage wall!

It was humbling to see the mural through my adult appreciation. It was not "just something hanging on the garage wall."

On the lower-left corner, Dad signed his name in large letters and the year 1944. It was his memorial for the veterans of World War II. No memorial could be more appropriate to honor the veterans than this mural titled *Suffer The Little Children To Come Unto Me*.

Life in New Jersey

If I had to live my life
over again,
I'd be a monk
because they have all the
time
in the world to do what
they want.

First Baptist Church: Montclair, New Jersey

Dwight James Baum designed a new addition to the First Baptist Church in Montclair, New Jersey. He got me back again from Mizner. See, I was back and forth all the time, and it was interesting. Of course, I had to take the wife and kids, too. That made it tough for the kids–school and everything.

I painted some murals with F.M. Lamb up in Stoughton, Massachusetts. We had the job of painting murals for the church, full-sized murals. A minister from England, by the name of T.R. Glover of Cambridge University, helped me with the subjects of the murals. Biblically, I didn't know much, but he did.

They had one stained-glass [Tiffany] window in the chapel. We did a mural above that. The murals were twenty-eight-feet long and about seven-feet high, and they were painted on Irish linen. Underneath was Gaelic writings. Beautiful lettering–took forever to do them. Most of it was in twenty-three-carat gold leaf, beautiful stuff. The monks used to do it years ago.

If I had to live my life over again, I'd be a monk because they have all the time in the world to do what they want, with no worry about taxes, clothing, food...nothing. They got their loaf of bread and a bottle of wine a day and did what they wanted. Now what the hell more do you want? Can you imagine anybody giving you a place to sleep, feeding you, and giving you a nice big bottle of wine every day? Nothing in the world to worry about, nothing. But that's the reason they did such beautiful work–total concentration. That's what made them so successful.

This church–[First Baptist Church] in Montclair...I've got to tell you this–had to be restored years afterwards in the 60s. They had a rain leak in the roof and water damaged the murals. The minister, Albert B. Cohoe, was a fine friend of mine. A scaffold was put up, and I was to restore the murals, see. Well, they had a fellow in the church, and he was against this buddy of mine, the minister. He did everything in the world to get him out of that church, everything.

So on this mural of The Sermon on the Mount, *I had a life-size Judas standing behind Jesus. So I changed the face of Judas a little bit and gave him a good sneaky eye. It was a close resemblance to the Judas of the church.*

What Dad didn't tell in his oral history was that while he was thirty-feet high on the scaffold, he altered the face of Jesus to resemble that of Jimmy Paton, the much-loved, Scottish janitor of the church.

The Black Cat

Dad and the workmen would sit on the steps outside to eat their lunch. It seems that an annoying black cat got into the church, and one of the workers striped the cat from its nose to the tip of its tail with orange paint, then carried him outside during lunch break. He released the cat in front of a lady walking down the sidewalk. She stopped and exclaimed, "Oh, what a beautiful cat!"

The Church Interior

There is extensive stenciling on the exposed beams in the main dining hall and also in the library with colorful designs on the ceiling between the beams. Throughout the church the walls are stained and stenciled, with parrots being a major motif.

Murals

The murals that Dad mentions in the Montclair Baptist Church are priceless. The following photographs in this chapter were taken by Dallas Holsten.

Christ Washing the Feet of the Disciples

This mural has the following Gaelic inscription:

> Receive not Glory from men. How can ye believe who receive Glory one of another, and the Glory that cometh from the only God ye seek not?

Birth and Manger

This mural is inscribed:

And seek not ye what ye shall eat and what ye shall drink neither be ye of doubtful mind.

For all these things of the nations

Seek ye his Kingdom and these things shall be given unto you.

Sermon on the Mount

This mural is inscribed:

Ye know that they who are coming to rule over the gentiles, lord it over them and their great ones.

But it is not so among you. But whosoever would become great among you shall be your minister. And whoever would be first among you shall be in the service of all.

The Good Shepherd

This mural has a shepherd and lambs. The signature of F.M. Lamb, Dad's mentor, is appropriately located under a large lamb. It bears the following inscription:

I have come not to destroy, but to complete.

Tiffany Windows

The Tiffany windows appear to be three panels, The center one portrays Christ. The two end windows are decorative and have an inscription from John 14:6:

I am the way, the truth, and the life.

At Home in New Jersey

In 1928 when our family moved from Florida, we lived in a second-floor apartment on Monaque Place in Montclair, NJ, and became active members of the First Baptist Church.

Upon completion of the three-year decoration of the church, Baum sent Dad to decorate the New York YMCA and the Anthony Campaiana Mansion.

A Return Visit

In the early 1990s, I revisited the First Baptist Church. The church of my youth no longer existed. It had become a total structural disaster from years of serious water leakage. The church millionaires of my youth, who could easily manage the tremendous expense of operating the enormous facility, had died. Lack of funds and years of neglect in every area were evident.

I returned in 1997 and met a young minister, Robert Zoller, who said that in August of 1994, Christ Church had the opportunity to purchase the 900-seat Romanesque cathedral. The First Baptist Church was sold and became Christ Church.

A general contractor was commissioned to repair major visible damage. They began repair work on the library ceiling, but stopped when they discovered stenciled art covered with 60 years of accumulated dirt and soot.

Finishing a Masterpiece

Christ Church located a company in New York that specializes in both the esoteric details of historic preservation as well as basic construction and repair work.

Their evaluation was, "View the project not as repairing an old building but as finishing a masterpiece. That's truly what this building is."

Reverend Zoller said, "The church is listed as a historic facility with the state of New Jersey, as having Tiffany stained glass windows, hand-stenciled woodwork, and beautiful walls and ceiling murals. However, the fine craftsmanship of these items were covered with years of age and neglect. Part of the renovation process has been focused on bringing in artisans and craftspeople to restore the items to their original state.

"In the library soot was painstakingly removed by hand, then washed down using a gentle chemical solution.

"The murals were cleaned inch-by-inch with a special material imported from Germany. The Gaelic lettering was touched up with gold paint; gold leaf would be too expensive."

Dad always said, "If it's gold leaf, real gold, and you rub the gold leaf between your fingers and it disappears, that's proof that it's genuine."

That's true. Gold leaf comes in very thin sheets. Dad would have the plaster or wood painted with a special adhesive and when it became the proper sticky texture, the 3 x 3-inch thin sheet of gold would be applied and feathered with a soft brush. A larger size would be too difficult to work with.

The Skinner organ was not salvageable and was replaced by a sound system to accommodate a full orchestra that plays everything from Bach to Boogie.

Reverend Zoeller and I covered every square foot from the choir loft to the basement exchanging information. Three years of renovation and a million dollars gave a rebirth to a building now called Christ Church Cathedral.

Memories

I spent an hour alone in the sanctuary to savor the past and appreciate the present.

Waves from my past flowed over me:

- Dr. A.B. Cohoe's animated voice delivering sermons from the Bible beyond my youthful understanding. These became a blessing later in my life when they were desperately needed.

- My baptism in the tile pool, perhaps at age 10. I thought at the time, "How much deeper will this water get?" My true concern was, "How much higher will my gown float?"

- How Dad drove the family to Sunday-evening service in a truck that could accommodate himself, Mom, and Hannah on the front seat. The back of the truck had grilled sides, a roof, and a tailgate; Dad installed a drop-down, wooden seat for me. Winter or summer, I rode in the back.

The fact that we were the only family in the church who didn't have a car never crossed my mind. If anything, it made us luckier than the ones with uniformed chauffeurs who drove families to church in spit-polished limousines. Dad was always the one asked to deliver unneeded furniture to less fortunate families, and I could ride along.

On one delivery, we ended up on a dirt road and found a man and his wife with three kids, the youngest being a baby in diapers. They had a hole dug for a cellar, an old wooden table and several broken chairs were on the ground above the hole.

After Dad and the man unloaded the truck and placed the furniture on the ground, the mother insisted we join them for lunch...a big pot of cold, mashed potatoes already being devoured by flies.

Tramp Artist: The Life of Robert Webb

I wasn't hungry but sat with the family as did my father. When the mother shooed the flies by waving a sopping wet diaper over the mashed potatoes, Dad stood up and announced, "Thelma, we better leave. Your mother is alone."

During the long drive home, Dad repeated over and over, "The poor devils don't have anyplace to put the furniture. Goddamn, we're lucky!"

Dwight Baum, Dad, and the congregation of the 1930s would rejoice in the renewed warmth and beauty of what is now Christ Church Cathedral.

Childhood Recollections

Jail House Stone--the Best Basement in Town

*Dad was the captain of the family
and demanded and received
the impossible from each member.*

I n 1931, the First Baptist Church was completed and Dwight James Baum was remodeling the Fairholm estate in Newport, R.I. for Count and Countess Villa. He contracted Dad to decorate Fairholm.

Years later, I discovered a collection of 28 letters in their original envelopes, tied with a faded blue ribbon. These letters, some of which appear in "Love Letters" on page 159, provide a glimpse of the love that existed between my parents.

My Early Years with Dad

Dad and his Irish buddy, Charley, finished their day's work and stopped to have a few drinks at Turner's bar. When the pair headed for home they got involved in an auction in Verona, New Jersey. Dad threw in a few bids for whatever was being auctioned and became the owner of the old Verona stone jailhouse that had to be removed from its site within a short time.

To save face, he drove from the mountain top of Verona, down the valley, and over to the opposite mountain in the country town of Cedar Grove and purchased land on the dead end of Rugby Road, a short street with a steep hill. The left side had a house at the foot of the hill, another perched on the hilltop. Six homes were scattered on the right side with five vacant lots between Dad's and the first neighbor.

With a lot of sweat, swearing, and long hours, Dad hauled the jail stone-by-stone to Rugby Road to build "the best goddamn basement in town."

The building of "the best goddamn basement in town" was delayed as Dwight Baum commissioned Dad to do decorating on *Fairholm* in Newport, Rhode Island. In one of Dad's letters to Mom he mentioned payment toward the newly-purchased property and how they would be living in their own home by Christmas.

In May of 1931, the Newport work was completed and Dad, with the help of his father (Robert, Sr.), began building the Cedar Grove home. There were no blueprints, a sketch on notepaper worked fine.

Grandpa Webb could neither read nor write, but was a mathematical genius. I remember watching him lie on his belly to eyeball the level of the dirt in the basement hole. He'd direct the man with the horse pulling a wooden drag-scoop to go deeper to the right, left, or center. The dirt was dragged out and up over a little embankment that eventually became steps leading into the basement with a bulkhead door.

When Grandpa decided the basement was level and deep enough, the Italian immigrants mixed cement in a trough using a hoe, then shoveled it into a wheelbarrow, pushed it down the bulkhead, and poured it on the dirt to create a basement floor. A slow process.

Next came the basement walls using the jailhouse stone. Dad's words were, "I knew damn well these stones would do the whole basement. By God, the walls are 18 inches thick!"

The first floor was laid, then studs for rooms were hammered in place. Grandpa Webb hand-hewed every ceiling beam by stepping each foot inside an empty nail keg, then sliding a 2 x 4 beam between the two kegs and chipping both sides of the 2 x 4 with a sharp ax. Wide, pine boards became the ceiling for downstairs and the floor for upstairs.

The fireplace wall in the living room was sparkling, colored stone from Pennsylvania with a small window on each side.

Home in Cedar Grove

In the fall of 1931 we moved in among saw horses, wood chips, and wet paint. We lived on the first floor and were big shots because we had yellow fixtures in the bathroom and one slab of white marble (leftover from a job) for the floor.

Hannah and I shared a double bed in the second bedroom and fought each night about who had a foot or arm extending in the other's area. Dad came in one night, pulled the covers off, twisted one blanket into a rope, centered it down the middle of the bed and said, "You each stay on your own side, and I don't want to hear another damn word." Then we fought as to who caused the problem.

It was a cold winter. The floor furnace in the living room did little to heat the house. The marble on the bathroom floor was freezing cold on bare feet, and Hannah and I never stopped bickering.

Spring brought improvements. Radiators were installed, a coal furnace purchased, tile blocks covered the marble slab and the unfinished kitchen floor. The upstairs attic was roughed-in for two rooms. Hannah had the front end; I had the back.

For years Mom warned anyone going up or down the steps, "Be careful, the bottom step is higher." This was the result of a few inches left over from a wrong calculation when the steps were built. The extra inches were added to the bottom step.

Captain Dad

Dad was the captain of the family and demanded and received the impossible from each member. Mom was no exception. Many mornings I heard, "Rosa, get out of that bed and fix my breakfast. That's your job."

Cruel? No...It was this demanding that kept Mom an active part of the family.

The first summer in Cedar Grove, Dad taught me more lessons than I cared to learn. Hannah, in hysterics, tattled that I had something of hers. Dad appeared, "Does that belong to you?"

"No."

"Then why do you have your hands on it?"

I returned the object to Hannah and stood alone in shame and guilt.

I rebelled about house chores. Dad said, "You get in there and help your mother." Help I did. Saturday morning bed sheets were changed. The top sheet became the bottom, and a clean sheet was tucked in on top. Downstairs was cleaned on Saturday; upstairs on Thursday evening. Scrubbing the kitchen floor meant kneeling with a bucket of water, a scrub brush, and a rag to wipe up soap and water. Occasionally, Dad placed a nickel in a corner.

Mom became the envy of the neighborhood wives–she didn't have to empty the pan of water from under the icebox. Dad fixed it with a hose that led the melted ice directly outside.

I didn't know my mother was different from other mothers until we went shopping and the clerk was helping Mom try on dresses. She approached me, a second grader.

"What's the matter with your mother?"

"Nothing."

"Yes, there is something wrong with her."

"No, there isn't."

Parkinson's disease was not an issue in the family. Mom was *mother*, period!

A Hanging Strap

Dad controlled me in my rebellious moods by making verbal statements. Mom strapped me one time on my bare legs using a leather belt. With each stroke she wept, "This hurts me more than it hurts you."

Dad, who was watching in the background, hung the strap on a nail in the kitchen, "Rosa, it's here in case you need it."

Obviously, they were a team pitted against a smart-aleck. From that day forth, all Mom had to say was, "Do I have to get the strap?"

Boys Are Different

That first summer was also the summer I discovered there was a difference between boys and girls. The local boys dammed the brook in the woods to make a swimming hole. I had a perfect view of the skinny-dipping boys from my second-floor window. This discovery I decided to keep to myself.

A School Lesson

The Cedar Grove school had eight grades, each with a majority of first generation Italian pupils who came on buses, mostly from Little Falls and Singac. I soon learned the word *guinea* and proudly used it at the supper table.

When the word *guinea* was released from my potato-filled mouth, Dad dropped his knife and fork on his plate and reached over and removed the fork from my hand, "And what are you?"

How did I know what I was? No one ever told me.

Faster than I could swallow the potatoes, I learned that I was nobody any better than anybody else and what I was, was no fault of my own.

Whenever I stumbled for an answer to a question, Dad solved the problem in a hurry. "Out with it." Or, "When you're spoken to, you answer." The most dreaded was, "Out with the truth, and be quick about it."

Sunday Specials

Sunday's preparation began Saturday night with a bath and laying out clean clothes for church and Sunday school.

Dad drove Hannah and me the 15 miles to the First Baptist Church in Montclair for Sunday school and church. He didn't drop us off, he stayed. Mom attended only the evening fellowship. There was a light supper followed by a fireside sermon from the minister. Dad explained, "It's too difficult for your mother to be ready in time for the morning service."

Sunday afternoon was the treat of the week: a ride in Dad's new car. Good behavior was rewarded with a ten-cent *Good Humor* bar from the ice-cream truck parked by the Montclair golf course.

One Sunday, we headed to Bear Mountain in New York to meet Scottish friends for a picnic. Mom was sporting the latest style hat with a brim that covered the left side of her face. Suddenly Dad reached over, grabbed her hat, threw it out the window, "God-damn it, Rosa, I'm not talking to a hat!"

Mom responded, "Oh, Bob."

I giggled as she watched the hat rolling down the mountain.

The Hindenburg

Dad made a special trip with Hannah and me to see the Hindenburg dirigible float by Eagle Rock on its way to Lakehurst, New Jersey, where it was due to end its overseas journey.

It was exciting to see the gigantic balloon gliding through the sky, and Eagle Rock offered a perfect panorama view.

We returned home eager to tell Mom about the Hindenburg. Instead, Mom met us in the driveway to say the radio was giving details about the Hindenburg exploding and people dying.

Of course, we didn't believe it; we had just seen it.

The Egg Omelet

Due to Mom's health, Dad did the grocery shopping and a good deal of the cooking. Making bread was a family tradition.

Once he needed eggs and sent me to the A&P, the only grocery store in town. As was customary in the 1930s, the dozen eggs were placed in a paper bag. I chose a short cut through the woods to return home and was wildly swinging my arms when the bag of eggs hit a tree. I slowed my pace, dreading what Dad might say.

With fear, I handed Dad the slimy bag and waited. He sized up the situation, grinned, and said, "Rosa, we won't have to crack the eggs for the omelet. Thelma's already done it for us."

The Red Coat

Late one fall, Dad came into the living room holding two winter coats that Mom had worn for several years. He handed Hannah the beautiful, bright-red coat that had a white, fake-fur collar and specks of black and white in the red fabric. With joy, Hannah tried it on, and it fit her. She was now the proud owner of the coat I had always loved.

Dad then held the ugly, gray coat with narrow stripes of brown woven in the fabric. It had wide cuffs that ended with big, pointed wings sticking out. There were two patch pockets on each side, one opening above the other, and a big, wide belt with a huge buckle. Even folded over, the collar sat high on the shoulder. I hated that coat whenever my mother wore it.

Dad held it, "Thelma, try this on."

It was a baggy fit until Dad wrapped and buckled the wide belt around my waist. I glanced at Hannah smiling in the beautiful, red coat that fit her perfectly.

Mom in the Ugly Coat

I stood in the baggy coat and proceeded to have a temper tantrum. "I don't like it. I hate it. I won't wear it. Why can't I have the red one?"

When I exhausted my tantrum, Dad calmly said, "The red one fits Hannah, and this one fits you. If you don't like it, you don't have to wear it."

That last sentence made me feel better until he added, "A coat is only good for one thing and that's to keep you warm."

Dad hung the coat in the front hall closet, and the subject was never mentioned again. He had given me the choice to wear or not wear it. In silent anger I thought, "I am not going to wear it."

However, when the snow came, and icicles hung from the gutters, I changed my mind and wore the coat...without the belt.

Off to Florida

Dad's work was always slow during December. The day school closed for the Christmas holidays was the day we would depart for our annual visit to Grandma and Grandpa Webb's in Lake Worth, Florida. Preparations for the journey, as in previous years, began the day after Thanksgiving when Mom started packing. What few clothes we had disappeared piece-by-piece in cardboard boxes. By departure day, the only clothing we had left was covering our bodies.

The year of Hannah's red coat and my ugly coat was the same routine as previous winters. The packed boxes were stacked on the back seat by the right window. Hannah sat in her red coat by the left window, and I squeezed between her and the boxes wearing a sweater, not the ugly coat. My unspoken choice was not mentioned by anyone. There was no heater in the car. Mom and Hannah wore coats. Dad and I wore sweaters. Dad had no coat.

Another subject not mentioned was my tendency to be car sick. Really car sick!

When we reached U.S. 1, Mom made her annual statement, "Now we stay on this road all the way to Lake Worth. It starts in Maine and ends in Miami."

We didn't get out of southern New Jersey before my car sickness was ready to be realized. I leaned toward the front seat grunting with a mouth full trying to attract Dad's and Mom's attention.

Hannah ordered, "Sit back and stop moving around."

I turned toward Hannah–my mouth opened and showered the beautiful red coat...fake-fur collar and all.

Hannah screamed, "Thelma threw up on me!"

Dad pulled to the side of the road and Hannah, still yelling, got out dripping with vomit. Dad stepped toward me and gently wiped my mouth with his handkerchief. Then, turning to Hannah he attempted to clean her coat saying, "She didn't do it on purpose. Stop your fussing."

Hannah, Dad, and I returned to our seats. Dad started the motor and Mom, who stayed in the car uninvolved, said, "I'll open the window a crack."

When I think back, throwing up on Hannah and the beautiful, red coat is one of my happiest childhood memories.

The unhappiest also involved driving to Florida each Christmas.

Mom, whose biggest joy in life was to be in the car riding, spent her time sightseeing and asking Dad questions.

Tramp Artist:: The Life of Robert Webb

"Bob, I smell rubber burning. Do you have the brake off?"

"Yes, Rosa."

"Bob, do you have enough gas?"

"Yes, Rosa."

"Bob, I think we should have turned right back there."

Dad's patience decreased as Mom's questions increased...then the explosion came. The car came to an abrupt stop off the edge of the road, Dad would reach across Mom, open the door and order, "Get out! Get to hell out and walk!"

Mom never budged. In her southern accent, "Bob, I won't say another word."

I sat quietly on the back seat visualizing my poor, sweet mother left in the backwoods of whatever state we were in. One year it was the wilderness of Georgia, and we had just passed a road gang of prisoners working in the woods with big, iron balls chained to their ankles and wearing horizontal-striped coveralls and a round, striped pillbox hat.

Mom would repeat, "Bob, I promise, I won't say another word."

He would reach across Mom, slam the door, "Make goddamn sure you don't."

We'd drive for a quiet few miles, then the silence would be broken, "Bob, did you take the brake off? I smell rubber..."

The only other stop was for gas. Dad tended to the car while Mom, Hannah, and I headed to the ladies' room. Whether we had to go or not, we went.

Mom returned to the car and Dad said, "You girls walk down the road and I'll pick you up."

We always believed him, but shouldn't have. We walked, ran, and skipped down the road trying to out-do each other. Dad would approach, toot the horn, pass us, then stop ahead and wait for us to run to catch up. We'd almost reach the car and Dad would drive forward, stop and wait. This continued until we were panting, begging for mercy, and be so exhausted we'd be content to sit and not argue for a couple of hours.

Christmas in Florida

Christmas in Florida was always exciting: aunts, uncles, cousins, Grandma's murphy bed, the ocean, and waiting for Santa Claus. What more could a kid want?

The ten grandchildren of the senior Webb's sat cross-legged in a circle on Grandma's living-room floor, each waiting for his or her name to be called for Santa's present. I received warm slippers. And a new dress–well, new to me. Cousin Shirley and I always received hand-me-downs from an older sister. I, from one sister; Shirley, from four. I hated my plaid dress as much as Shirley hated her blue smocked dress. With our mothers' permissions, we exchanged ownership of dresses. That made Christmas truly merry.

Except for the addition of grapefruit and oranges, the return to Cedar Grove was much the same as the journey to Florida. However, one year, state inspectors stopped vehicles to remove all fruit because of some kind of bug.

Dad was furious, "The bloody state encourages people to spend money buying fruit so they can make money, then they take it away. You kids start eating."

Home Life

The Webb house was always neat and clean. There were no knick-knacks, just paintings hanging on all the walls. Major cleaning was in spring when Dad removed everything to the front yard, furniture, rugs, lamps...everything. Draperies hung on the clothes line for fresh air. Then he cleaned the inside walls, windows, woodwork, floors–no wax to protect Mom–then each piece of furniture was returned to the inside, after it was cleaned.

For a week following the big cleaning, Dad walked around the house inhaling deeply, "Everything smells so clean and fresh. Isn't it nice?"

Charley Arrives

One spring Dad's sister, Jane, in Florida, shipped me a colorful Bantam rooster named Charley. Charley slept outside on my second-floor bedroom window sill. When winter blew a blizzard one night, Charley became frozen in a block of ice.

Dad came to the rescue with an extension ladder and placed the ice block–with Charley in it–on top of the radiator. Ever so slowly the ice melted, and Charley's body was covered with towels, my tears, and Dad's assurance, "He'll be alright."

Charley came to life minus his fancy comb and acquired a Rhode Island Red girl-friend, Susie.

We'll Fix That, Rosie

When Mom's Parkinson's disease reached the stage where she tripped on the oriental rugs,(acquired as a trade-off for art work) Dad said, "We'll fix that, Rosie." He rolled the rugs and stored them in the garage, leaving the floors bare.

As Mom lowered herself to sit in a chair, she couldn't bend her body as others do. She'd flop in the chair, causing it to slide on the bare floor and out from underneath her. Dad said, "We'll fix that, Rosie."

He walked to the garage, returned with a hammer, and nailed all the furniture to the floor.

Trading Tops

The kitchen had a porcelain-top table and an old, oak unit complete with a flour bin and a pull-out, wooden table-top. One evening Dad and his buddy, Charley, were sitting at the table drinking and talking. They sat for hours until Dad said, "Damn, Charley, this porcelain top is cold. Now if we take the wooden top off that unit over there and put this porcelain top on, then put the wooden top on these legs, it would be a hell of a sight more comfortable. Let's fix it."

Mom said, "Oh, Bob."

Hannah, Mom, and I went to bed, leaving Dad and Charley alone to drink, talk, and make a lot of noise. The next morning there was no sign of Dad or Charley but there stood the wooden top on the legs that had supported the porcelain top, and the porcelain top now appeared on the old, oak Hoosier unit. No one said a word about it, and that's the way the table tops remained for the next 35 years.

Looking back, I realized many of Dad's "fix-its" were supported by alcohol. Mom never condemned or argued about his drinking.

If Dad didn't return from work when expected, Mom, who was a walking telephone directory, would say "Thelma, call 10266 and ask if your father is there." From memory Mom could recite the telephone number of every barroom within a 25-mile radius.

I gave the operator the number, then asked whoever answered the phone if Bob Webb was there. The person answering the phone would yell, "Bob Webb here?" Without exception the response was, "NO! No Bob Webb here."

Immediately, Mom recited another number.

After a few phone calls, Dad arrived home. "What the hell are you calling me for, Rosa?"

Look It Up

No matter what level of communication Dad adopted, Mom remained calm; however, she had one weapon she'd use to defeat him.

Because her right hand trembled from Parkinson's disease, she was unable to write, but as a speller she was unbeatable. Dad did the letter writing to family members, but he was a poor speller.

"Rosa, how do you spell...?"

If Mom was on good terms with Dad, she'd provide the correct spelling. If annoyed, she'd say, "Look it up in the dictionary."

"How the hell can I look it up in the dictionary if I can't spell it?"

"I don't know, Bob." The joy in her voice could not be mistaken.

The scene would end one of two ways. Dad would walk from his desk too angry to continue writing or he'd burst into laughter. "All right, Rosa, you win. How the hell do you spell...?"

Hobos

I was the one to help Dad unload paint buckets and drop cloths from the truck when he'd arrive home from work. It didn't take long for me to learn to have the wind on my backside before shaking the drop cloth.

On Saturdays he'd take me on a job that often led to side adventures. Once he parked the truck along a country road, "Come on, Thelma, let's see what we can find."

We followed a brook in a field, "Look! Watercress! We'll pick some for supper."

Another time Dad parked by a pond and taught me how to tie a nail to the end of a stick and gig frogs. The lesson included cutting the legs off and throwing the body in the pond for the fish to eat. At home we floured, fried, and ate our adventure, which Hannah and Mom thought disgusting.

One side trip meant parking the truck off the road, putting groceries and beer in a box, and dragging them down the railroad track–a long distance for short legs. Following a path in the woods led to a group of shabbily dressed men. One with an amputated arm, one minus several teeth his buddy had pulled out with pliers. All with a hardy welcome for Dad and his kid.

The long, empty sleeve dangling fascinated me as did the tooth-pulling pliers resting on a rock.

I was impressed when the men showed me how to place some grocery items in the nearby brook for refrigeration. I sat on a rock listening in pure joy while Dad and the hobos drank beer and told stories. It was a disappointment when Dad refused their offer of food, "We have to get home."

Walking back on the railroad tracks he said, "Poor buggers need the food for themselves."

Hot Temperature

Late one winter, Dad and Hannah became seriously ill with pneumonia. We put them in the twin beds in our parents' bedroom and had a registered nurse, Jean, attend them. It was a stressful time for all–and Dad, not accustomed to being sick, had little patience. He bargained with Jean, who was newly engaged to be married, that if she'd get him on his feet in a hurry, he'd build her a house.

She put a thermometer in his mouth, turned, and did the same to Hannah. While she was tending to Hannah, Dad, feeling mischievous, quickly dipped his thermometer in the cup of hot tea sitting on his night table, then returned it to his mouth. Jean removed his thermometer for a reading and said, "Oh, my God!"

Dad was so pleased with her reaction that he couldn't stop laughing long enough to tell her it was a joke... Jean whipped the covers off, rolled him on his side, and stuck the thermometer in a more reliable location.

Dad played no more pranks on Jean.

A Promise Kept

In the early spring, in good health and being a man of his word, Dad started building a house for Jean and her husband-to-be.

Days were warm, but frost still threatened at night. The day the basement cement was poured, Dad kept a barn fire burning the entire night. His buddy–me–accepted the invitation to join him. Hot dogs, marshmallows, beer, and soda tasted extra good in the cold air.

Bantam Charley and Rhode Island Susie discovered that the construction of a house offered great places to roost. Judge Haller was the town judge and also a crackerjack plumber whom Dad hired to install the plumbing. He started the job in good faith then approached Dad in anger with a Judge's order, "Who the hell can work there with chicken shit all over everything? Clean up the shit or get another plumber."

Dad laughed and started the clean-up and because the chickens belonged to me...

The bride and the groom moved in. They had so many children they had to find a larger house. A young, Jewish couple asked to rent the house. Dad agreed. However, the neighbors complained about the prospect of having Jews in the neighborhood. Dad approached the couple, explained what was going on, and said, "It's up to you. If you want to live where the neighbors don't want you, it's alright with me."

They chose not to move in.

Graduation

Eighth grade was the time for graduation and change...some students went on to high school, some to vocational school to learn a trade, and some to work with no further education. Graduation was important for those not continuing on to high school.

Girls were dressed in long, pastel-colored dresses they made in sewing class. Boys were dressed in their best clothes, some even wore suits and ties!

The graduation celebration was a bus trip to the affordable Wedgewood Cafeteria in Montclair. During the course of dinner, a florist delivered a box of red roses, one for each student and teacher. This was an exciting surprise, and no one knew who sent the roses.

Days later, Mom gave the secret away...it was Dad. He never mentioned roses, nor did he ever learn Mom had tattled!

My Teenage Years

Dad had his own way of handling Hannah's and my teenage years.

When his 17-year-old nephew left Florida to learn the paint trade from Uncle Bob, he was not allowed to live in the house with Dad's blossoming daughters. Uncle Bob found him a room in Verona.

High school for Cedar Grove kids meant a long bus ride to Bloomfield. Few students owned cars, and I felt fortunate to be offered a ride home in a fellow student's dilapidated car. I had no intentions of telling Dad, but blabbermouth Hannah did.

Dad raved, "I'm paying taxes for the bloody bus, young lady. You ride the bus both ways. Don't you get in any car."

Big Band

Frank Daley's *Meadowbrook* was a classy, nationally known club in Cedar Grove where the big bands played and broadcast their music on radio.

With the understanding that we would be home by 10 PM with no *if*s, *and*s, or *but*s, Dad reluctantly gave permission for Hannah and me to go to the *Meadowbrook* with a group of other teenagers to listen to Tommy Dorsey. The ten o'clock curfew passed without notice. When the clock struck eleven, the *Meadowbrook* had a rumpus with some man walking among the tables in his pajamas looking for his daughters.

Dad found us.

Life in Williamsburg

*So the future
may learn from the past.*

–John D. Rockefeller, Jr.

Portrait of John D. Rockefeller, Jr. and
Kenneth Chorley, President of Colonial Williamsburg (by R. Webb)

The country was still in severe depression, and to earn a living Dad was house painting–inside and out–and wallpapering. Many of his jobs came from church members.

In the late '30s while living in Cedar Grove, New Jersey, he found a new job–he commuted to New York City to be in charge of maintenance for a Park Avenue apartment. It was during this time that he was being interviewed in New York for the possibility of a job in Williamsburg, Virginia. He accepted an offer for a six-week trial period.

Fortunately it was summertime and, as he said, "I stayed in a room over a garage with a basin and toilet in the room and a cold water shower downstairs in the open garage. It seems I was always in a garage–at Ringling's too."

When Dad completed the six-week trial period, he returned to our home in Cedar Grove, New Jersey, and wrote the following letter to Mr. Chorley, President of Colonial Williamsburg:

Mr. Kenneth Chorley

Williamsburg Restoration, Inc.

Williamsburg, VA.

July 30, 1940

Dear Mr. Chorley:

I want to thank you for your time the other afternoon.

I was deeply moved with your interest and feeling to the extent of consideration due each man. For the first time in my life I have the pleasure of working for a company that instructed or even gave me wholeheartedly the privilege to do for a worker that which I have always considered he was entitled to. You and Mr. Holland can be assured that each man will be helped and given every opportunity to hold his job as long as he works under me.

I am very proud of the paint department equipment. I intend to care for it as though it were my own property, and with it I am sure that the highest quality work can be done at a reasonable price.

I like Williamsburg very much, and the work is interesting. I enjoy working for Mr. Holland and the Restoration in general.

If the three-month trial, which is about up, has proven satisfactory to the extent of steady employment, I will do my best to live up to expectations. If it has not, I thank you for three pleasant months' work.

Very truly yours,

Robert Webb, Jr.

On the Move

Dad talked endlessly about the very real possibility, if he was accepted, of moving to Williamsburg for a new job, a regular one that, "...my God, pays fifty dollars a week...a steady paycheck!"

Dad was accepted to be in charge of the Williamsburg paint department. There was no hesitation about leaving the Cedar Grove home he had built. It was rented. He soon found a bungalow on Capitol Landing Road in Williamsburg and prepared the family to move.

The Tramp Artist and his family were on the move again.

Basement Packing

My contribution toward the move was to sort and to pack the accumulated stuff in the basement. I had one box for packing and one for trash. Being an immature teen-ager, I was in a hurry to get the job over with. I wanted to drive my boyfriend's convertible with my newly acquired driver's license.

More stuff was flying into the trash box than into the save box. I noticed a roll of tissue paper with a rubber band that protruded from the trash box and was about to shove it down in the box when I saw markings on the paper. I removed the rubber band and discovered several sketches in neat rows. They were unfinished and nothing that Dad would have drawn. So I rerolled the papers, bent them in half, and threw them in the trash. But they popped up again, and something told me to take them out. I pitched the roll into the Williamsburg box.

When I began to unpack the boxes in Williamsburg, I was once again confronted with the roll of tissue-wrapped sketches. I flipped the roll in the corner of the dining room where Dad had stacked his artist's supplies.

Some months later Dad spread the sketches on the dining room table, carefully stroked the wrinkles from the tissue, and silently studied each sketch.

Quietly he said, "George Inness started an art colony in Montclair. He was considered the best landscape artist in the country. He'd walk in the woods, make sketches on paper, then do paintings in his studio from the sketches. These are more valuable than the paintings." I never confessed.

In 1997 I made an appointment with the registrar at the Virginia Museum of Fine Arts in Richmond, Virginia, to see the George Inness sketches Dad had donated.

The associate registrar met me by the information booth and led me into a secured area where priceless items were stored. Stopping at her desk, the registrar slipped on a pair of cotton gloves, then carefully lifted the lid on a cardboard box that held the sketches.

I stepped forward to study the sketches. There were nine drawings on each sheet in rows of three–postcard size–separated by an inch. I couldn't decide what medium Inness had used, perhaps oil. Each had varied tones of brown, olive, and sepia. As I focused my attention on the sketches, they came alive in movement and feeling–tiny birds flew, lakes rippled, trees swayed. I felt each could stand alone as a finished landscape.

I stood in reverence several minutes and recalled my teenage ignorance. George Inness almost didn't make it to Williamsburg!

Sketches by George Inness

A New Home

Summer was the ideal season to move to Williamsburg. It allowed time to settle in the rented bungalow on Capitol Landing Road, explore the area, and make plans for fall.

I registered at Matthew Whaley School for my senior year. Mom, a born southerner, felt at home before the dishes were in the cupboards.

Hannah was accepted at McMaster University in Canada. She returned at Thanksgiving with the desire to be a nurse and became a student at Buxton Hospital in Newport News, Virginia. A location convenient for home visits.

Bantam Charley and his companion, Susie, adjusted well to their new, fenced-in backyard. However, a neighbor complained about Charley's cock-a-doodle-doo at sunrise. To keep goodwill, Dad located a farm willing to adopt Charley and Susie. I accepted this knowing that Charley would strut his charm, and Susie was too old and tough for stewing.

I learned the few motels available in Williamsburg were unable to accommodate the influx of tourists, so I registered at the Tourist Bureau and rented out my bedroom. I willingly slept on the living-room sofa. It was an easy way to make the extra money a teen required.

Dad was busy and happy organizing the paint shop.

Capitol Landing Road was a good start for life in Williamsburg.

Palace Farms

In 1941, Dad moved Mom and me from the bungalow on Capitol Landing Road to a two-story colonial house behind the Palace across the railroad tracks. There were just three houses on the acreage referred to as Palace Farm.

I wanted the first Christmas in the new home to be special and asked Dad for a tree.

"I'll get you a tree when the time comes."

Time was drawing close and I reminded him of his promise. Dad responded casually, "Don't be in such a hurry. You'll get your tree."

Christmas Eve arrived, the boxes of ornaments and the tree stand sat on the living room floor–with no tree. My Christmas spirit was low. I wouldn't even speak to Dad.

Dad gleefully went to the basement, returned to the living room, walked past me with a saw in hand, and ran up the stairs. A few minutes later he was stomping down the stairs singing, "Here comes Santa Claus, here comes Santa Claus!"

Dragging behind him was a Christmas tree, perfect in height and fullness. Santa grinned, "Does this suit you?"

Mom said, "Oh, Bob, you didn't!"

"Sure as hell did. I've been waiting to cut the top off that bloody tree ever since we moved in. It won't keep me awake scratching on the window anymore."

It was our last Christmas together as a family.

World War II

The United States had declared war. Hannah was in her second year of training at Buxton Hospital. I had graduated from Matthew Whaley school and was earning $12.50 per week as a telephone operator in Williamsburg.

War changed Williamsburg dramatically. The main road from Williamsburg to Yorktown was closed to the public. Camp Peary was being constructed by the Navy Seabees. Servicemen from the Seabees, the Navy, the Marines, and the Army arrived, along with hundreds of civilian workers from the Newport News shipyard.

A drastic shortage of living accommodations caused people to rent their spare rooms to out-of-state workers or servicemen and their wives who were on a few days leave.

The switchboard at the telephone company was in a constant state of emergency as it became the connection to the outside world. There were eight- and ten-hour delays on any long-distance calls because the government had priority for the lines, and its calls were numbered in priority order of 1, 2, or 3 to Washington, D.C. Operators worked endlessly.

Our family rented our third bedroom to two men working on the construction of Camp Peary. It was not unusual for servicemen to knock on people's doors and ask for a place to sleep. Once, a sailor knocked and Dad said, "The only place we have left is the dining room floor."

The sailor answered, "I'll take it."

He slept on the floor two nights and ate a hearty breakfast each morning. Maybe that was the beginning of the bed-and-breakfast phenomenon!

Many Changes

Hannah eloped with a tonsillectomy patient and was expelled from the nursing school. Married students were not allowed. She and Russell lived in a tiny bungalow in Newport News close to the shipyard where he worked as an engraver. Eventually, he became a sailor. Hannah and their baby, Mary Lou, moved in with Mom and Dad. Hannah became a much-needed night telephone operator. She tended to Mary Lou during the day, tucked her in bed for the night, and then went to work. What she didn't know was that Dad would take the chubby, cute grandchild out of the crib to spoil her.

He used the excuse, "The kid will sleep late in the morning, and Hannah can catch up on her sleep." It worked.

I decided to join the Navy Waves, and I asked Dad to sign a consent form because I was under age.

"Damndest idea I ever heard of. No decent girl would join the Navy. No, I won't sign."

Not long after that, John Wright and I decided to marry. Again, Dad's permission was needed because I was under age.

"Hell no. If you're smart you'll join the Navy, meet interesting people, and see the world."

I lied about my age, eloped, and moved to Richmond. John was soon drafted into the Army. I didn't return home, but talked Dad into renting me the garage apartment in Cedar Grove, New Jersey. There I awaited the birth of my baby. The rent was twenty-five dollars a month, my income as a service wife was $50. The first month I sent Dad an $18.50 war bond with a note saying if he held it to maturity, it would be worth the $25 he charged for rent.

When the baby was due, Dad left Williamsburg to be with me. I woke him in the wee hours of the morning on July 10th, "Dad, we better go to the hospital."

He raced through red lights beeping the horn in a fast, non-stop ride to the Montclair Community hospital. I was wheeled to the labor room, and Dad was escorted to a waiting room reserved for expectant fathers, or in our case, grandfathers.

During his waiting period the nursing staff had a change of shift, and Dad became the forgotten man.

"Christ, everybody in New Jersey and Virginia knew Sherry had arrived before I did. I think John got his V-mail in Germany while I was still waiting!"

Dad returned to life in Williamsburg, and I continued to send him a war bond to cover the monthly rent.

Soldier and Sailor Returns

When World War II ended, Russell returned to Williamsburg to join Hannah and decide what to do about their future. During the time Russell was in the service, Hannah had the privilege of buying groceries at the PX. On each shopping trip she bought a six-pack of beer and stored it in the basement, projecting on Russell's return. In civilian grocery stores, beer was hard to come by. When she went to the basement to present her gift to the returning sailor, she discovered the beer in the cans had been siphoned off, replaced with water, and carefully sealed. It didn't take much detective work to declare the sailor from World War I guilty without a reasonable doubt.

Hannah approached Dad in a rage.

"Huh?"

Mom said, "Oh, Bob! How could you?"

Russell had a great story to tell for years.

Russell and Hannah rented the main house in Cedar Grove, and Russell, having learned engraving in the Newport News shipyard, bought one machine and started engraving on a new material–plastic. His engraving company became the second largest in the United States. They eventually moved to Oklahoma, half-way between the east and west coasts, where he had business contracts.

Hannah and Russell had two more daughters. A blonde and a redhead joined Mary Lou, the brunette.

My husband returned from Germany. We left New Jersey and returned to Richmond, where John continued his career with the telephone company. Sherry became big sister to brothers, Bill, Bobby, and Jimmy.

With the war over and his daughters building their own families and lives, Dad was getting restless. He bought an acre of wooded land on Neck-O-Land Road off Jamestown Road on the outskirts of Williamsburg.

A new life for Mom and Dad began on Webb's Acre, and his accomplishments with the Williamsburg Restoration continued until May 1962, when he retired.

Restoration Years

The pastor of the Bruton Parish Church in Williamsburg, Dr. W.A.R. Goodwin, dreamed of a revival of colonial Williamsburg. This dream, combined with John D. Rockefeller, Jr.'s interest and money, gave a rebirth to Williamsburg. The restoration began in 1928 and, by the time Dad arrived in 1940, the American public had already become aware of the importance of restoring the Colonial Capital. Curious tourists traveled there to see what was developing.

For thirty years, Rockefeller, Jr. contributed the funds necessary to remove the 19th-century houses and buildings so that reconstruction of the 18th-century houses and buildings could be on their original foundations. It was a slow, ongoing process because many of the properties were purchased by giving life-rights to those in residence.

Restoration in the '40s

In the early '40s, Williamsburg had three distinct groups of people: William and Mary faculty and students, the Restoration people, and the original Williamsburg families. This combination had little in common, yet each realized that it would be to their mutual benefit to cooperate with the monumental changes in progress.

Dad's contribution to Williamsburg is best told through his own oral history and through the interviews I had with people who worked for him.[1]

Colonial Williamsburg asked the National Lead Company to recommend somebody as a color maker and superintendent for the restoration of colors for Colonial Williamsburg. I suppose they interviewed some before they did me; but, anyway, the National Lead Company recommended me for the job. Elton Holland hired me in New York City with the approval of Mr. Chorley, who at that time was President of Colonial Williamsburg.

I came here in 1940 and took over the painting and color making. That's when we used to make all our own colors and paint. They don't do that any more. Different companies had the right to make the Williamsburg colors. I think it ended up now that Martin-Senour has it all. Things have changed so much.

My interest here in the first place was the authenticity of colors: Your blue, your yellow, and your red: which are the three primaries. At one time, that was all there was: blue, yellow and red. And from that you had seventeen secondary colors, which were made from the intermixing of the three primaries. From those seventeen secondary colors, Sing Moorehead and I arrived at authenticating about sixty of the colors that were used by the settlers of Colonial Williamsburg because they didn't waste anything. If they had one of the primaries and another one, they mixed them together, and that's how they got these very deep, rich colors. There's no way in the world to create any more colors than existed here.

We authenticated them, and they had records of the colors. They still do. I think they kept the original colors in the restored buildings that are seen by the public.

When I first came here one man told me, "So-and-so lives over there, the house is painted. The only house in town that's painted." The scraping down of that house– now Bassett Hall–revealed an original yellow ochre. Yellow ochre is one of the primaries, and Bassett Hall was colored yellow ochre. Then they applied white over that, which we didn't have. The only white we had was whitewash over a color, possibly, but not white paint. It just didn't exist until the white lead came along, and then they had a white they called colun that's mined in Colun, North Carolina or Colun, Georgia. And that's used for pastels–chalks. School chalk is made out of colun. It's surface mining. You take the top soil off, and then they dig up this white stuff and that's colun.

---

1. Robert Webb's transcript provided courtesy of Colonial Williamsburg Foundation Archives, Oral History Collection, "The Reminiscences of Robert Webb," 1976.

Yellow ochre–there's one place in Rhode Island they call Ochre Point. When the tide goes out or used to–I suppose it's all gone now–they used to spade this yellow clay up in blocks, take it ashore, dry it and pulverize it, and mix it with linseed oil. That was your yellow ochre. It's a very hard paint. Two or three buildings had it on for a time. Bassett Hall had it, and we had a terrible time getting Bassett Hall white because we had to burn that old ochre off. Hard as iron.

And then the red was Spanish red, came from Spain, most of it. Some from Italy. That was a primer, and a lot of buildings were left red. Lots of buildings were yellow. There were a lot of them blue. The Blue Bell, for example, was blue. The blue comes from Cobalt, Ontario, Canada. There's a whole town up there that manufactures cobalt color, dry. Then the manufacturers put it into oil and make paint of it. The colder a country is, the better the blue is. It has a deeper hue, the colder it is. Siberia has the most beautiful cobalt and that's a very brilliant blue, and that's mined. So the primaries that's mined is your cobalt blue and your Spanish brown. Some people call it Indian brown. In some parts of the country they call it Venetian red, but it's still the same pigment. Yellow ochre is surface mined. There's only the three. The old portrait painters only had those three colors to work with. That's the reason the old masters are so dark in color, they had to use what colors they had.

For the buildings that are open to the public, the colors were authenticated by pieces of wood that we had left over and cleaned them down. Some of them had eight or ten coats of paint on, some more. You'd have to take one coat of paint off and then leave what was there and keep on going, just like steps, until you had gone all the way back to the original colors, and then you could see what they'd done. Most of them were Spanish brown. Once in a great while you'd find one with yellow ochre or a cobalt, but not very much. But everything was primed with Spanish brown.

Of course, they used a lot of fabric in those days, too, you know. Mrs. Nash was hired for decorating–she was from the office of Perry, Shaw, and Hepburn of Boston, Massachusetts. She did a lot of decorating here. She was a very brilliant woman. She decorated the original Inn years ago. She favored wallpapers and marbleizing. She was a wonderful woman and knew her business.

She'd give me a piece of wallpaper and say, "Now, get something as close to that as you can." So I'd go down to the shop, and I'd make it up. She was always happy about the results. She'd pick out the predominate color of fabric or wallpaper and that would be the color of the wood. And the ceiling would be the lighter part of the fabric or wallpaper. Even if the job was just finished today and furnished, you'd think it had been done years ago. The Inn and rentals had a homey atmosphere the day they were finished.

There was a couple of places she ran out of wallpaper and couldn't get any more. Then I'd get the colors together and go over and paint the wall to match with the wallpaper. It was a lot of fun.

There was sort of a paint lab when I got here. They'd been working with Singleton Moorehead and another man. They used to make samples and put it in quart cans and put it on shelves. But canned paint doesn't stay up. Materially speaking, it's alright, but the color goes, see. One color eats up another when you get away from those three primaries. Use straight cobalt and it'll be cobalt a hundred years from now. It will be yellow ochre a hundred years from now. And it'll be Spanish brown or Venetian red forever, if you don't do anything else with it. It's when you intermix them, that's when you get your trouble because one will eat up the other.

When you mix a pot of paint using the three primaries or the secondary colors and you don't keep a formula for it, the next time you mix it, you'll end up with something different even if you weigh it out by the hundredth part of an ounce. You've got to use it the way you did it first, or you'll end up with a different hue every time. One will eat up the other. Then you'll be scratching your head trying to figure out what happened.

Living Quarters

When I came here, God, I stayed in a garage–I always was in a garage, at Ringling's too–I stayed in a garage by the Kerr House, down by the Capitol.

Well, there was a garage around the corner that was supposed to have been an authentic garage of Colonial Williamsburg. After they found out it wasn't, they moved it down to the Palace Green. I lived in the upstairs, and there was a wash basin and toilet up there, that's all. Downstairs, a garage with no doors on it and a thing that you pulled for a shower. Cold water. For some reason or another, every time I was down there taking a shower in this cold water some neckers would drive in the yard and park. So there I was.

Mrs. Christian lived in the house with her son. He graduated from William and Mary. He was a tall, fine fellow. Thelma came down to visit me and Mrs. Christian says, "Don't stay there where your father is. Come over to my house." She was a good-hearted ole girl. They had three floors to the house, and on the third floor there was two bedrooms and a bath. Thelma was staying in one of those rooms upstairs, and she went into the bathroom to have a bath. No lock on the door or anything. The son came home unexpectedly and walked into the bathroom and found her in the tub without a damn thing on, see, and she let out a scream. She didn't even know there was a man in the house!

Well, things were different then. The natives were different. The more the public came in, the more closed the doors got. There was something about it years ago... I remember one house on Duke of Gloucester Street. It's on the right-hand side across from Judge Armistead's house, standing on the corner there, the Taliaferro-Cole House. There used to be a woman who lived there, and her husband was the doctor of the nuthouse. There were quite a few steps to get to that door of the house. I went up there one time when I first came here. I thought, well, this must be one of the Restoration houses. And it had a sign on the door, "Nosey!"–and the tourists would go up and look at the sign and come down laughing. It was a private house. Well, those things are gone.

Peyton Randolph Nelson

They had cows in back of the old courthouse. The man that owned them lived over back of where the Lodge is now. He had a big house, Tazewell Hall, next to Bassett Hall, Rockefeller, Jr.'s house. Old Nelson. Peyton Randolph Nelson. He owned them, and he walked around all the time in his undershirt with suspenders, dungarees, and cowboy boots. They couldn't do much with him because he'd refer to a law they had that all public greens were grazing greens for anybody's cattle. He had ducks and geese there too. He just put back what used to be there. He was a bird, that fellow was.

The Restoration bought his house, but he had life-rights to live there. The Restoration was responsible for major repairs so he just let minor repairs grow into major repairs.

I went to visit him several times. You ought to see this house, Tazewell Hall. That was a nice old house. He ate canned goods and opened the cans and threw them on the floor where he was. He was a dirty, old bugger with a long beard. Yet he was well liked by the people that lived here, the older people. The older people were one family, see, all one family.

Pulaski Club

The Armistead sisters had two brothers that were lawyers here and there was Judge Armistead that I knew very well, the old man. I don't know his son too well; I've met him. His son has been here, and Mary, his daughter, when she was a little kid. I gave her a couple of my paintings. This present judge and his father used to sit on the bench down on Duke of Gloucester Street at what they call the Pulaski Club. I used to stop there and chew the fat with him. He's quite a character, the old man was.

That was a private club, they had no building. They just sat down on the bench and if the weather was bad they'd go in the Cole Shop there.

It was one bench that way and one this way, see, and that was their club, and it was right across the street from the Judge's house. They were all big shots. I don't know what Pulaski means. It was an old social club, not many members. You had to be invited to join. The membership fee was four dollars and a bottle of bourbon. The membership card was handwritten on an Octagon Soap wrapper. When Mr. Rockefeller, Jr. joined, he borrowed four dollars from a member and had his chauffeur deliver the whiskey because he was a teetotaler. [the Pulaski Club still has benches on the main street.]

Well, all the tradesmen were mostly local people. They were honest people: carpenters, fishermen, and farmers. Most of them were in-laws or out-laws of the families that owned the properties here, so when the Restoration bought properties, there were relatives, so they got them a job. So you had to make mechanics of them, that's all there is to it, see. With the exception of very few, they all turned out to be very decent people and damn good mechanics when they had somebody to instruct them, and they didn't mind being shown, told how to do things. They were very acceptable to it because it was their job, and they all turned out to be good. I didn't have any trouble except with one or two, that's all.

One time I had about twenty-eight painters, good men. Some of them are still working here.

Carriages

Well, they were authenticated designs of the family. It's a coat of arms. And the crest. The coat of arms is one thing, then the crest is another, and the crest is part of the coat of arms. I know nothing about the College of Heraldry, which is in [Edinburgh] Scotland. It's known all over the world.

Carriages are still built. It's a lifetime job. In Greece when a daughter was born, the old royalty would start right away building a carriage for her wedding gift, and they'd hire the carpenters, the blacksmiths, they'd breed the horses, they'd make the harnesses and it would take until she was married to complete a carriage. They looked like jewels, and they still have them in Greece and Portugal. Beautiful. God, they're beautiful!

Here, [Williamsburg] we did most of it Sundays—the varnishing and the striping— because I couldn't stripe with a shop full of people. You weren't allowed to be near the old stripers. Even the automobile stripers years ago, they were mostly women, you couldn't go in where they were striping. You'd break their concentration.

I couldn't do that kind of work in the shop. I could do the priming and the sanding and the rubbing down with pumice, but the actual decoration and striping I used to do nights down there and Sundays. The wife used to go down and read to me while I was painting when it was quiet and no dust, which made it nice. I didn't know what she was reading. I didn't pay any attention to that, but, never the less, she was reading. It was nice for me to have somebody with me. Those days are gone.

You can't get the materials. Coats of arms and striping are Japan colors. They're not oil colors. Japan colors are a dried pigment that you use with Japan, which is a liquid. Japan is made from burnt varnish and then mixed with turpentine, and it's ground in a mortar and pestle.

Signs

I did all the original signs. I don't want to underestimate those who made it possible because it took a lot of historic information and know-how, and it took a lot of work by the architects. We had one man who went to England and took photographs of different old signs. The same man designed and built the windmill. There's a lot involved prior to painting. I dare say any sign painter today could do what I did, as far as the signs are concerned, because the patterns were all designed for size of the panel and then you perforated the outlines.

Old Sing Moorehead and I would get together on the colors and I'd paint them. So I wouldn't say there was too much about it other than just painting them. I don't want to take somebody else's credit because there's a lot of people involved. It's like everything that's done worthwhile, there's a lot of people involved. It isn't just one man.

Palace Coat of Arms

When I did the coat of arms for the Palace, Ed Kendrew says, "How long is that going to last, Webb? It's costing a fortune to do it."

I said, "It's going to last about twenty years." And I'd have bet on that.

So when it was time to do it again, he says, "I have a note that you said that coat of arms would last twenty years. It's only been eighteen years."

That's it, eighteen years. So that was that for the Palace coat of arms.

Another fellow came along and did it. It's nothing unusual about it. It's just experience. But the architectural work is what made Williamsburg, I'll guarantee that. You wouldn't have nothing here if it wasn't for the man with the pen, nothing. You wouldn't have had a Palace, you wouldn't have had nothing because it takes an architect to put it on paper. Then it takes mechanics and good supervision. There's nothing worthwhile done alone, nothing, not a damn thing.

The colors of the interior of the buildings were always decided on before I got to the job. We authenticated the colors before there were any buildings built, really. Then the colors of what we authenticated were approved by the decorator or the architect's office, then we proceeded on that basis. I didn't go into what you call the Raleigh Tavern and say this is the Raleigh Tavern blue.

I didn't decide what was going to be what. I did make the colors and I saw to it that they were applied properly. That was my end of it. It's the same with the signs, same with the carriages. There were a lot of people involved besides me, so I'm not trying to build up the idea that I was the only one because there's no such a thing as one in Williamsburg, never was.

Marbleizing

The marbleizing at the Inn, I did that on my own. Mrs. Fisher and I was over there and I said to her, "What are you going to do with all this beautiful art you've got here? And the baseboard?"

She said, "What would you suggest?"

I said, "How about letting me marbleize it for you."

She said, "That would be wonderful. I wouldn't dare mention it because I didn't know you could do it."

So I marbleized the Inn area and it has become one of the outstanding spots of color.

I marbleized a few fireplaces, Raleigh Tavern, Allen Byrd House, the Lightfoot House.

Marbleizing is really something. There are thousands of marbles, thousands, and they come from all over the world. Now the marble in Georgia is black and white and in different parts of the world the marbles are different colors. Now in the Inn, the marbleizing is Lavanta marble, which comes from Italy, originally. Of course, it's paint here.

You've got to have an awful good surface in the first place, and you've got to pick out the color for the background, the predominating color, which you're going to do. The predominating color is the background, and over that you start washing in the colors of the marble. Most of them have a predominating color for the background, some's white, some's yellow, some's blue, some's red; and you wash them in. Then after they're dry, you have to varnish them to give them a gloss.

Stenciling

Dad used his stenciling skills extensively in churches and homes on the East Coast. There isn't a great deal of stenciling in Williamsburg.

The stenciled floor in the Carolina room at Abby Aldrich Rockefeller Folk Art Collection–I did that. I didn't do it alone. A sign painter helped. I cut the stencils. It was copied from a painting in the room, Boy With Finch. I cut the stencils with a stencil knife. I put the paper down and cut them on glass. The stenciling was done on raw wood. We stained the floor first, and then we put the stenciling down. Gave it three coats of a very hard type of varnish, cosmo spar varnish. You could have a horse dancing on that floor! I told them not to wax it because wax over that kind of varnish is a solvent. Wax softens the varnish.

Restoring

I did a lot of work at the Abby Aldrich Rockefeller Folk Art Collection (AARFAC). I did the Indian as you go down the steps that's hanging on the wall. It's the bow from a ship that is done with English, that is, red English mercury. It's a dry pigment that I ground with oil. I did it out in my barn. It's the same mercury that is used in red inks even today. You get it from sheep bladders. The bladder of a sheep is a little bigger than an orange. They put this dry powder in there, and the weight of it, the size, is terrific. It's as heavy as lead and very expensive. That's what the bow's red is, it's made out of mercury which is a permanent material. They all went wild about it. They can't replace it.

I worked on some Indian figures for the Jamestown settlement. My barn studio was full of paintings to be restored from New Jersey, North Carolina, and Maryland. They were sent to me, and I restored them.

This man, Fred Hewitt, we'd been friends for years. He called me about a painting by Warr, a world-known marine painter. Somebody had varnished over one of his paintings, and the varnish had alligatored. So Fred took it to New York, and they just simply couldn't do nothing. Fred told me there was nobody up there that dared tackle it. So I said, "Well, I can't do any worse."

He brought it down, he and his wife lived with me for two days. He got me a whole bolt of cheesecloth down at Casey's department store.

I removed the varnish off the painting, and I didn't interfere with the painting at all. I was very fortunate because it had been varnished by Warr many years ago, and the varnish had gone flat. The sheen was gone, but whoever varnished it after that had put on a high-gloss varnish that dried fast and that was what had alligatored. All I had to do was remove the varnish. I had good luck with it, and Fred got a great kick out of that.

At that time Rosa was in Montclair, New Jersey, for a serious operation. A very dear friend of Hewitt's was a surgeon. He took care of her. When the job was finished, I took the painting back to Fred in my car and we were discussing the cost of doing things. I told him, "Your doctor friend charged me seven hundred dollars for Rosa's operation. I think that's ridiculous."

He said, "One profession to another," and gave me the same amount. It saved the day for me.

At one point, I talked with Floyd Martin who had this to say about Dad's restoration work:

I think about the best one I've seen him do in restoring was two paintings that were in a hen house down at the Morecocks Restaurant. The rats had eaten about half of them away. It was of the Portuguese fishing camps. It had the piers and fishing nets-- all of that was missing. He painted all that back in it, and the net looked like it was a net just sitting there, had all the little holes in it. I tell you right now, it was the pretti-

est thing you ever saw. It was covered with chicken manure and everything else–you couldn't even tell what it was. He could transfer an old oil painting from rotted canvas onto a new backing and hand you the rotten backing. Unbelievable.

My wife and I would take Bob and Rosa down to Sarasota in the wintertime and go down in the spring and drive them back. A nice trip, fresh fruit off the trees and we'd ride around down there and go different places. Just a good time we had with them.

Once we went to the Ringling Mansion. We went into the dining room and joined a tour group, and they had all these oval designs painted on the ceiling over the dining room table. The guide told how the artist did it, laying flat on his back. We were listening to the guide tell about the designs coming from Mrs. Ringling's collection of cameos and somebody asked, "Is the artist dead, or is he still living?"

The guide said, "Oh, no, he's been dead for years."

We got to laughing, and I looked at him and said, "Goddamn, you're doing pretty good for a dead man!" I never will forget it. Must have been twenty people in that group.

Bob said, "Well, I hate to tell you, lady, but I'm the man who did it."

Then everybody started talking at once. They all wanted to ask him questions about who painted this room and who painted that room–all the way through. I found out...I didn't know there was an American gold and an Italian gold. Italian is darker. The cornice in some of those rooms is different. I asked him why one was lighter than the other. He told me one was Italian, the other was American. I didn't know that.

In the course of researching this book, I had the opportunity to speak with many craftsman who had worked for Dad during the Williamsburg project. What they had to say appears in "Remembered by Others" on page 169.

Coach Detail

Dad continued his story, telling of the coach decorations:

Just after I left Sargent and was waiting to join the Navy, I went to Reading, Massachusetts, North Reading. I painted and decorated carriages. The horse and wagons that the fruit dealers and vegetable people had. They had panels all around the wagon, the loveliest paintings of fruits and vegetables you ever saw in your life. God, those things would be worth a fortune today.

I painted all these panels of fruit: pears, grapes, and vegetables. They were beautiful. And I striped them, too. Of course, that's why I got so much work done in Colonial Williamsburg on carriages, see, I had worked on wagons and stuff like that. What a life that was.

Some Coach Signs

- Randolph... (formally Goode Coach), Williamsburg green. Payton Randolph coat of arms. Seats four, no more. For public use.

- Landau...Golden background. Squirrel and coat of arms. C.A.A. (Carriage Association of America) 1st. place 1994. Seats four to six. For dignitaries.

- Mulberry...Maroon. Sociable or called Blue Phaeton design. Seats four to six. Public use.

- Wythe...(formally Lafayette Coach). Mustard yellow. George Wythe coat of arms. Seats four. For special events

In 1998 Philip Moore said, "When repainting is needed, I do the decorative work, not the basic painting. I do pinstriping, scrollwork, and coats of arms. Most of the original patterns that Mr. Webb used were worn out and the paper dry rotted. We get new copies from architect's original drawings. They keep a master copy."

Pictoral Signs

The painting of signs, coat of arms at the Palace and Capitol, marbleizing at the Williamsburg Inn, stenciling in the Carolina room at the Abby Aldrich Museum, plus the art work and striping on the carriages were subcontracted by Dad. He did many of the jobs evenings and weekends. If the work was portable, such as the signs, he worked in his home studio.

The Williamsburg pictorial signs held a special place in Dad's heart. In his oral history he acknowledged he painted all the original tavern signs but, "The research done by the architects made it possible."

Signboards had an important purpose. They depicted the service or product a shop offered. Pictures and symbols substituted for written words as many people were illiterate.

- The King's Arm Tavern represented food and drink.

- The Boot and Shoemaker shop made and repaired boots and shoes.

- The Raleigh Tavern, famous for food, drink, and politicians, offered sleeping quarters for weary, male travelers. They shared one large room.

Tramp Artist: The Life of Robert Webb

- The Millinery Shop, which has oval portraits of the owners, Jan and Margaret Hunter in gold frames mounted on the gable, each wearing a stylish hat of the period.

- The Chowning Tavern, a favorite of Dad's. Josiah Chowning, with a smile of anticipation, is pictured drawing the cork from a blue-green bottle.

- The Hunter's Store sold pork products, thus the sign of a ferocious pig running.

- The Golden Ball represented a goldsmith jeweler.

- The Cabinetmaking Shop has a picture of a Chippendale side chair with a red, upholstered seat.

- The Apothecary Shop depicts a haystack, which was the surname of Peter Hays, who owned the shop.

- Pasteur-Galt, a second apothecary shop, has the druggist's mortar and pestle.

- The Tailor Shop of Severinus Durfey is represented by a hanging lamb, a symbol of wool and tailoring.

- The Silversmith Shop is depicted by a loving cup with a cover that kept flies out of the wine. And appropriately painted silver.

Portraits of prominent people were often used. There are about 23 pictorial signs in the restored area of Colonial Williamsburg. Some of these signs appear in "Glimpses of Williamsburg" on page 197.

Recognition

Dad received many commendations for his efforts at Williamsburg, some of which appear in "Awards for Work at Williamsburg" on page 189.

Six months before Dad's retirement from Colonial Williamsburg, he received an invitation from the Virginia Chapter of The American Institute of Architects to attend their banquet and receive an award for outstanding craftsmanship in the field of architectural painting.

Life as Work

I must go to the store
and get some crackers and cheese...
I can't afford to live here
and eat here too.

Boot jack made by Bob Webb
(He couldn't afford to subcontract!)

Governor's Mansion, Raleigh

Dad phoned his 13-year-old grandson and namesake: "Get your mother to bring you down here. I've got a marbleizing job you can help me with, and you can learn something worthwhile."

The teenager recited the learning experience, "Mom, I slept in the balcony, and early the next morning Gramps and I went zooming to Raleigh at about 85 miles an hour.

"We went to the Governor's Mansion, and the governor's wife led us to one of the bedrooms on the second floor. We were going to marbleize a fireplace and mantel. We plastered the fireplace bricks. Gramps said it had to be a perfectly smooth surface. Then we left to spend the night in a motel to let the plaster dry.

"The next morning we returned and primed the fireplace with a couple of coats of latex paint. Gramps said it dries fast. The vertical area had to be green, and the horizontal section cream.

"After lunch it was dry, and he let me brush boiled linseed oil onto it. He showed me a brush with long, thin bristles and said, 'Bobby, this is a lettering brush. I'm going to lay in the color for the marbleizing. It will bleed into the linseed oil and feather out and not leave hard lines. It'll dry smooth like real marble.'

"Gramps was talking about marbleizing all the other fireplaces. 'This was just a sample, a freebie.'

"Later, when I asked Gramps if he was going to do anymore fireplaces he said, 'No, the cheap, bloody politicians wanted something for nothing.'"

Old Salem, North Carolina

In 1963 a letter was sent from Old Salem, North Carolina, to Colonial Williamsburg requesting information about a man qualified to do fancy marbleizing at Old Salem.

The response was:

> We highly recommend Mr. Robert Webb, who formerly was Superintendent of the Paint Shop for Colonial Williamsburg. He is now retired and enjoys traveling around the country, and he is interested in some specialized jobs such as this one at Old Salem and is qualified and experienced in this field."

On May 17,1964 I received the following letter from Dad written on Holiday Inn stationary:

Dear Folks,

Well, here is where we live and expect to be here until the job is finished, which will be about three weeks. I selected this place because there are no steps and I would not have to worry about your mother falling. Now that it is over, and all is well, I can tell you. The 3rd day on the job, the damn scaffold collapsed and down went Humpty Dumpty, paint and all. They took me to the hospital. Results were broken ribs, twisted knee, and plenty of bruises. There was no room in the hospital, so they sent me here. Your mother and friends, including the Martins that used to live next to us on Jamestown Road, took care of me. I was back on the job on Monday. I fell on Wednesday 1 P.M... I am wearing a corset, but there are no garter catches for my stockings. I am doing very well.

We like it here for a change. It is very expensive, but we are comfortable. There won't be much money left on the job but why worry. Jim Dodson of Martin Marrietta, took us to his place on the lake Saturday and out to dinner, then home. I told him we enjoyed the day, but I could see why their damn stock was so far in the rear. He said wait a few months. He reminded me I was paid the same interest regardless of stock value.

Well, I must go to the store and get some crackers and cheese. I can't afford to live here and eat here too. I will stop and see you all on the way home next month.

Love to all,

Mother and Father

I was surprised to read in *The Richmond Times Dispatch*, June 3, 1973, about Dad having a lawsuit against Old Salem:

> A skilled painter specializing in restoration of Colonial buildings won a federal court ruling Thursday ordering a lower court to determine damages due him because he fell while working on a project in North Carolina.
>
> The 4th U.S. Circuit Court of Appeals said Robert Webb Jr. was owed damages by the Old Salem Inc., a Colonial township being restored at Winston-Salem, North Carolina.
>
> Webb, 66, was injured May 6, 1964, breaking five ribs when he fell six feet from a scaffold.
>
> Webb took the job for $100.00 a day shortly after he retired as director of painting and decorating at Colonial Williamsburg, Virginia. He contracted to do the work, with Old Salem, Inc. supplying the scaffolding.
>
> The court termed Webb no ordinary painter but a uniquely skilled artisan sought after for his expertise in restoration. The 4th Circuit Judges ruled Thursday that the case would be sent back to the lower court, which will determine Webb's damages and allow recovery from Old Salem.

As if it weren't bad enough for Dad to have his first job-related injury, he had to be involved with the two professions he hated with a passion: medicine and law.

What a pill to swallow!

The Chrysler

One weekend Dad and Mom drove to Richmond in a new Chrysler to visit me. The car was painted a dark green that became known as "Grandpa-green." Surprised, I asked, "What happened? Did you wreck the old one?"

"Nope, this was a gift from Mrs. Chrysler."

I shook my head, "Yeah, I believe that."

Dad grinned, "It's the truth. The last time I was working on their farm, Mrs. Chrysler asked me why I didn't have a Chrysler. I told her I couldn't afford one. She made arrangements and gave me this one. Nice, huh?"

I turned to Mom, "Mom, is he telling the truth?"

She laughed, "Yes. It's true."

Dad often talked about going to the Walter Chrysler estate in North Wales, in the foothills of Virginia. "They're real people. They do their own canning and make jams. God, what a place they have with horses and gardens. They are so down to earth. Mrs. Chrysler called me to do some work, and I told her I couldn't unless provisions were made for my wife. She put us up in a guest house and treated us like royalty."

They became friends and often exchanged telephone and home visits. Dad was proud of their friendship and of the "Grandpa-green" car. No vehicle received better care...even the engine was scrubbed and polished regularly.

On one visit I noticed adhesive tape over the gasoline gage and speedometer. "What's the tape for?"

"I got sick and tired of your mother telling me I needed gas and I was going too fast."

Homefront

Many of my friends in Richmond knew Mom and Dad. They never refused an invitation to visit Webb's Acre. I liked to travel scenic Route 5, the old wagon-road from Richmond to Williamsburg where many old plantations face the James River.

One summer day at the Webb's, my friend, Hawky, and I were sitting on the picnic bench just outside the kitchen door chatting with Mom and Dad. Dad excused himself and in a few minutes returned with a hammer in his hand and a baseball cap on his head. He sat and rejoined the conversation. Slowly and nonchalantly he bent over, hammered a nail into the outside of his left leg, removed his hat, and hung it on the nail. No one paid any attention, and the conversation continued. When the visit ended, he removed the cap from the nail, placed it on his head, and walked his visitors to the car with a limp.

As was customary, he stood in the driveway as the car pulled away and bid farewell by waving with a handkerchief in each hand.

A mile down the road Hawky, obviously puzzled, said, "I didn't know your father had a wooden leg."

I responded, "He doesn't."

Hawky pondered this a few seconds then said, "But he drove a nail in his leg!"

"Nah, the old fool slid a board down his sock to pull your leg."

"Except for your mother, your whole family is crazy!"

Lisp Kid

On another visit, Dad and I were sitting on the picnic bench beneath the kitchen window talking when a neighbor-boy appeared. A child of five with large, blue eyes and two front teeth missing, he opened his mouth to display holes the dentist left where two teeth had been pulled.

Dad angled the little chin so he could inspect the empty space. "Did you tell the dentist what I told you to tell him?"

"Yeth."

"What did you tell him?"

The child lisped badly. "I said, Mr. Webb said you are not a dentist but a horse doctor that puts shoes on horses."

"What did he say to you?"

The child continued in his tiny voice. "He said to ask you why you had to come all the way back from Florida to bug him."

Dad nudged me with his elbow, "Fetch an apple from the refrigerator and a piece of candy from the jar."

Returning with the goodies I overheard, "Did you put the turtle where I told you to?"

Suspicious, I asked, "What turtle?"

"He showed me a turtle he found in the woods, and I told him to put it in between the sheets in his father's bed, way down where his feet are."

I looked at the innocent child, "Did you do it?"

"No, I was scared."

I turned to the old man on the bench who was enjoying a hardy laugh, "You should be ashamed of yourself!"

I left him and walked in the studio. The work table was covered with rows of cast iron bootjacks. They were in a design representing a colonial man. Yellow devil horns protruding from the head gave a perfect oval space to grab the heel of a boot so it could be pulled off a foot. The men had green painted pants, a black jacket with yellow buttons, and a white collar.

I said, "Dad, I could paint these. Let me do it."

"I'm being paid to paint them, not subcontract them."

That was the end of that until I accidently learned he was paid 35 cents for each bootjack painted. He couldn't afford to subcontract!

No Show

Dad was excited when he received an invitation to have a one-man show and projected no problems about having enough paintings. He contacted members of the family asking each to loan him a few paintings. Not one positive response did he receive.

He raved. He pleaded. One niece suggested he take the refusals as appreciation by his family of his work. A young grandchild saw an opportunity to make a fast buck and offered to sell him one.

Dad wrote me:

> Everyone I gave paintings to won't let me have any back, not even for money. I offered Ruth [a niece] a hundred for the painting I gave her but she said, "No. Paint more."
>
> I can still paint so I will keep what I paint and sell when I can, so keep what you have. They are old and no good anyway.

The end result was no show.

Eventually he found humor in the rejection and loved telling the story of the show that could have been.

Was he generous with his paintings? Yes and no. If he liked a person, he'd give them a painting. If he didn't, he wouldn't sell them one.

He did have a problem quoting prices to prospective buyers, and there were some paintings he just didn't want to sell. I suggested he put a price sticker on the ones he was willing to sell and a sold sticker on the ones he wanted to keep.

"That's a damn good idea. I'll do it, and that includes everybody in the family. I've got too damn many relatives."

He did and, regretfully, that included me.

Bill by Hand

Dad sent handwritten, itemized bills to people who owed him payment for jobs. One man met Dad on the street, "Bob, the total on your bill was wrong. I owed you more and sent you a check. You haven't even thanked me."

"Why should I? You're the one who would have to live knowing you cheated me!"

Life Abroad

The Webbs are coming
to Italy!

Thelma, Bob, Hannah, and Ginny

I drove to Sarasota to surprise Mom and Dad. I arrived in mid-afternoon and found them sitting at their small kitchen table, both with pans in their laps and paring knives in their hands. Dad looked up, "Hi! Your mother and I are making peach jam."

Yes, they were. Dad had a pan full of peaches. Mom held a single peach. Dad didn't allow Parkinson's disease to exclude Mom in family activities. To Dad, Mom's one peach was more important than all of the peaches in his pan.

Holding back my tears, I joined the party, and with Mom's instructions helped until the melted wax was poured on top of the hot jam.

I looked at Dad, "So what have you been doing to stay out of trouble?"

Well, I went down to see Ringling Towers. My God, it's beautiful. I sit in that chair in the lobby and look up at those ceilings and I can't believe it. Because those colors have taken on all the richness that you don't get on a fresh job. They've taken on age. They go back to the original colors, the blues, the reds, and the yellows. In mixing with oils, colors change, but after a few years they go back to the earth color they came from. Plus the fact that when the job was done we used to go over it with cracked walnuts. The shells of walnuts, not the meat but the outer bark of the walnut. They used to pulverize it and soak it in milk–buttermilk–and go over it with that, add age to them. That ceiling today is something. Boy, that's a beautiful job.

Shortly after my Florida visit, I received a letter from Dad that read, in part:

If I can arrange it, I am going on a trip to Italy. Your mother said she would stay with Ada [a sister-in-law]. I will know in a few days. First, I must become a member of the Ringling Museum. At least I can dream.

Step-by-step the dream became a reality that included me, Hannah, and Hannah's friend, Ginny. The adventure was a gift to Hannah and me from the Webbs.

Italy Beware

The Webbs are coming to Italy!

The first art tour sponsored by the Ringling Museum was to be Italy, the country Mable Ringling loved and where she found many designs, ideas, and statues for Cà d' Zan.

Florence Gilmore, the organizer, said, "A hundred and thirty people. Too many." We were too much for Italy. They split us up on two buses. Our group went around Italy clockwise, the other group counterclockwise. The only time we met was in Florence.

While Florence coped with the usual–and unusual–problems a tour director has, I had my buddy, Dad, to supervise. Hannah and Ginny stayed together and were uninvolved in the events concerning Bob Webb.

Venice and Royalty

The tour followed the usual sights and wonders of Italy, but I was eager to see romantic Venice. Before arriving, the guide gave the usual facts: Venice is built on 117 islands and has 150 canals with 400 bridges. The arch in the center of the bridges is high enough for a gondola to glide through.

Our first evening was spent at St. Mark's Basilica feeding pigeons in the Square and sitting at a small, round table sipping wine while violinists serenaded us with romantic melodies.

In the morning, we toured the Palace of the Doges. A wonder of design for the average tourist to explore but for Dad it had personal meaning, "This is the palace Mrs. Ringling loved and used as a model and inspiration to build Cà d' Zan." He examined every archway, hall, and ceiling with reverence.

The following evening the group boarded a private yacht of Countess Gotsey for a party at her palatial home on a private island. Violinists playing lively Italian songs met the guests at the dock and led them to her beautiful garden where drinks were served. Dad had charmed the Countess and was asked to assist her in leading the guests across the first floor of the palace to a courtyard where tables were set with white linen cloths, napkins and two bottles of wine–red and white.

I sensed trouble. I maneuvered myself in the parade to be assured of a seat at the table of the Countess and her escort, Dad.

Unfortunately, a compulsive talker sat next to Dad. Dad's scheme to shut her up was to keep her wine glass brim-full, and it didn't matter which color–red or white; she downed each with equal fervor. Her husband leaned close to her ear and whispered, "Stop it" about the same number of times I nudged Dad to behave himself. Neither obeyed.

Florence later told me that the Count, who was short and did not speak English, sat next to her and spent the entire dinner pinching her behind.

The trio of violinists played while circling among the tables. After a dinner of several courses, served by white-gloved waitresses, the violinist, followed by the Countess and her jolly escort, Dad, led the group to the second floor. An orchestra was waiting to play for dancing in the main salon. From the salon opened a huge balcony where more drinks and food were available.

The Countess, who had recently had a cast removed from her broken leg, used a cane to help balance her six-foot frame. Dad, who never danced in his life, had the Countess dancing Webb style–walking straight ahead, then turning around and walking straight ahead in another direction. She had no cane for balance on the slick tile floor, just the fool that was walking forward and pushing her backward in all directions.

Wanting to be out of that scene, I joined the people on the balcony. Miss Wino, from the dinner table, was sipping more wine. She leaned backward over the balcony rail and her wig fell off. Dad and the Countess arrived on the balcony in time to see Miss Wino weave and knock over several beautiful flower pots from the railing. As they crashed to the ground, the Countess placed her fingers over her lips, "Oh, my poor babies."

Dad poked me, "Isn't that disgusting? Look at the manners on that woman."

The yacht returned our group to Venice, and we all retired to our respective rooms except Hannah and Ginny. They decided to go on a moonlight gondola ride.

I recognized the voice that went with the knock on my door, "Thelma, I'm in trouble. Open the door!"

I opened the door, and there stood Dad in his undershorts. He stepped inside my room giggling, "I thought there was an ice machine around the corner where I could get some ice fast. There is no damn machine! My door shut, and I'm locked out of my room. Do something!"

I phoned the front desk. Judging from the broken-English response I received, they were having trouble understanding why a man was locked out of his room and was waiting to be rescued in a room assigned to three women. Eventually, two men knocked on the door and escorted the barefooted, laughing fool to his room.

Early in the morning there was scratching on the door accompanied by the same rec-ognizable voice, "Thelma, I'm sick as hell. I've got diarrhea. We can't go back to Rome with the group today. I'm so sick I'm dying!"

In my nightgown, I walked him back to his room. Once again his door had shut, and he was locked out. We returned to my room–my door had shut, and I was locked out. Fortunately, Hannah and Ginny had not left.

The front desk sent the same two men to unlock the old man's door, who walked back to his room in his pajamas with me in my gown holding him up. He was terribly sick with a touch of diarrhea caused by a hearty amount of booze.

Hannah and Ginny, both nurses, joined the group leaving for Rome. That left me, who had no nursing talent, spending an extra day in Venice attending to the boozer. He slept soundly between his frequent trips to the bathroom. I confiscated the bottle and the keys to both rooms. When I thought the front desk had a shift of personnel, I phoned requesting information on when the train would leave the next day for Rome.

Early in the morning, the old man was fully dressed, sober, and eagerly looking for-ward to Rome. I was weary but anxious to be in Rome, back with the tour group. With the aid of the gondolier, we stepped carefully into the wobbly, local taxi service.

The gondolier, who did not understand English, stood high in the back with a long pole in his hand waiting for destination instructions. I obliged with a sound that I thought would be universally understood for the word *train*, "Choo-choo, choo-choo."

Fatso Dad, who was sinking the front of the taxi to water level, handed me a piece of paper he had been writing on, "Give the man this, and stop making a damn fool of yourself."

I handed the gondolier a sketch of a train. He smiled, nodded, and glided the taxi to the "choo-choo."

The train was on time and served a four-course, gourmet breakfast that improved my attitude considerably.

As we stood in the gigantic Rome *Termini* station, Dad turned to me, "Find me a toi-let, I've got to go bad. Hurry up."

I stopped the first man passing and spoke one of the few Italian words I knew, *toiletta*. He pointed at himself and said "French."

Dad said, "Hurry up. Don't be so damn slow."

I approached a woman, "*Toiletta*?" The woman, continuing to walk in a fast pace pointed to the right. We rushed in that direction. Dad ran in, and I stayed by the entrance to wait. Several women walked through the door... "Oh God, he's in the ladies' room!"

Dad made his exit, "Jesus Christ, there's a woman in there that hands you two pieces of paper. They don't have a toilet, just a round hole in the floor. Goddamn, I had a hell of a time."

A taxi drove us to our hotel to await the tour group.

Touring the Eternal City

A lifetime would not be enough to absorb all the wonders of Rome. Dad studied many paintings and, in some cases, knew more details and facts than the guide offered. I wondered where my father–with a fifth-grade education–acquired his knowledge of the old masters: their techniques and the schools of art they represented?

Florence gave our group a map and two free days in Rome to choose what we wanted to experience at our own pace. Dad's and my first choice was the Vatican. Dad covered every inch in awed disbelief. What magnificence!

We entered the Sistine Chapel and saw Michelangelo's masterpiece. My fascination of the Sistine ceiling began in grammar school. Now here I stood beneath it, and I couldn't look!

I turned toward Dad. He wasn't looking either. He placed his arm across my shoulder, "Well, Thelm, we didn't come this far not to look."

Slowly I looked to the ceiling and felt tears running down my face. I glanced at Dad, his tears were flowing. Our eyes met. I felt a warmth and closeness to Dad as our apprehension turned into unspeakable joy.

That afternoon, we walked among the ruins of the glorious Colosseum. A wonder of wonders, built how many centuries ago?

Dad quietly said, "I'd like to go back to St. Peter's tomorrow and see it again." We did and discovered much that we had overlooked on our previous visit.

We spent the return flight from Rome to Sarasota relaxing with thoughts of the past days and a desire to relive the journey. I gazed at Dad who was sound asleep and realized the trip to Italy was more than just sightseeing. Sharing the experience with Dad was the best part. I felt closer to him in both understanding and love.

Life in Marriage

...to hell with what people say!

The Webbs

The Webb marriage was always in a state of motion. Dad had home chores, work demands, endless energy, and a curiosity regarding all aspects of life. He also cared for a handicapped wife, whose jealousy had developed into a serious problem. He managed all this with his on-and-off drinking and the strong belief that "my marriage was made in heaven."

Difficult as the relationship was for them both, to Dad his Rosa came first. No event or honor bestowed upon him had greater meaning than their 50th wedding anniversary. To celebrate the occasion, Dad bought, wrote, and sent invitations to a dinner at the Cascades restaurant in Williamsburg. It was Dad who shopped with Mom to find the perfect, yellow dress for her to wear.

Hannah had family obligations in Oklahoma and was unable to attend. My husband was in a New Jersey hospital recovering from two serious heart attacks. Therefore, I was unable to help with the preparations of the celebration. However, Dad's grand-daughter, Mary Lou, who also lived in New Jersey, stayed with John thereby enabling me to drive to Williamsburg for the dinner.

I had purchased two gold cups and saucers for their tea during the dinner. It was a wonderful party: a friend played his banjo, and Dad gave a hilarious speech on how Mom survived 50 years with him.

When the party ended and I was preparing to return to New Jersey, Dad repacked the gold cups and saucers in the gift box and said, "I suppose you want these back?"

I understood his message and laughed, "Yes!"

"Well, take them now."

What's in a Name?

Less than a year after my husband's death, I was concerned about Dad's reaction to my forthcoming remarriage. I decided to phone and get it over with.

"Dad, I'm getting married."

His reaction was instant, "You're getting married? That's great! Now, Thelma, you're going to get a lot of lip from a lot of people but remember one thing. The dead ain't gonna be any deader a year from now than they are right now, and to hell with what people say."

The unpredictable Dad surfaced again when I was going through a divorce from my second, short-lived marriage.

He phoned me in my new apartment. "Thelma, I'm changing my will. What's your name this year?"

During the conversation Dad remarked, "A man of my world never receives recognition until after he's gone."

I sensed a sadness in his words. Later, as I was browsing through a bookstore I happened to spot *Twilight of Splendor* by James T. Maher. It describes many of the magnificent mansions in the United States, Cà d' Zan being one. What a thrill it was to read about Dad's contribution.

I bought the book and phoned Dad that evening and read a sentence: "Robert Webb, Jr., who was twenty-eight years old when he was put in charge of the decorative painting at Cà d' Zan was something of a rarity."

Dad interrupted, "Christ, it sounds like an obituary!"

Then he added, "I remember that fellow. He's a freelance writer. He talked with me about ten years ago and promised me a book. Write him and tell him I'm still alive and waiting."

"I bought you one and will mail it tomorrow."

"For the price of a postage stamp I might have gotten one free."

"Stop complaining. It's paid for."

A couple of days later, I phoned, "Did you approve of the part about you?"

"I haven't read it yet."

"I put in a bookmark so you could turn to it."

"I know. I decided to start at the beginning. I haven't reached the best part yet."

Tipsy-Topsy

I drove to Williamsburg to visit Dad and Mom before their departure to Sarasota for the winter. I entered the kitchen, and Dad was leaning on the stove stirring a large pot of stew with a long-handled, wooden spoon. "Where the hell have you been? I've been stirring this goddamn pot all day."

Mom said, "That's not all he's been doing all day."

"Christ, Rosa, I had to do something beside wait and stir this pot."

Dad was drunk. Somehow we got through supper. I then said, "I am going to spend the night in a motel."

Dad grinned, "If you think you can find a better place than this to stay, there's the door. Lots of luck, cause there ain't nothing available in Williamsburg this weekend."

He was right. I drove thirty miles to Newport News before finding a motel.

In the morning I returned to Webb's Acre. Dad was sober but not feeling well. "My knees hurt like hell."

Inhaling a deep breath for courage I said. "Dad, I refused to stay with you overnight because you were drunk, and it upsets me. Everybody in the family worries about your drinking. We all love you, but it hurts to see you digging your own grave with the bottle."

"Well, if I'm dead nobody will have to worry about me."

"Oh, yes we will. We'll worry about which way you're headed."

"Hell, you don't have to worry about that. I've got friends in both places!"

Back to Florida

Floyd Martin, as he had done for a few winters, drove them to Sarasota. I was concerned because Mom's health was at a difficult stage with no hope of improvement. For the past four years, Dad had given up painting in order to attend to Mom. He was determined to carry on alone in this no-win situation.

I phoned Sarasota. "Dad, how are you doing?"

There was silence, then with tears he said, "That's the first time anyone has ever asked me how I am doing. Everyone always asks how your mother is...no one ever asks how I am doing."

Having never before heard my father cry, I asked, "Dad, are you alright?"

"We're okay, considering. After all, no one can expect to live forever."

In early spring, Floyd returned them to Williamsburg.

Life in an Empty Nest

The only thing I can give my grandkids is memories.

New Shoes for All

S hortly after retirement, Dad and Mom drove to their Sarasota mobile home for the winter.

His way of adjusting to retirement is expressed in excerpts from his letters:

January 1, 1963

We are all settled here, and your mother is doing wonderful. It is rather cool here for Florida. I have lots to do, but I am taking it easy.

I have so many interesting things to do and no boss. It is such a relief to be on my own.

We wish you a very Happy New Year and good health. Don't take life too serious. We are dead a long time.

January 19, 1963

I don't think of how old I am. Maybe in another ten years I will think of my age.

I keep busy but don't work like I used to. My job for the day is to get all the bills paid and write letters. Also get the laundry done at the laundromat. I enjoy watching the people there. Some of the kids I could throw in the washing machine.

Let us know what day and time you expect to arrive. I will meet you. There will be some way for you to get around. There is a show place called the Cars of Yesterday close to our place. No doubt they will have a car for you to drive.

Mom and Dad were waiting at the airport when my plane landed. The weather was what is expected of Florida in mid-winter: warm and sunny.

One evening Dad walked to the side yard to check the number of grapefruit on his young tree that was now five-feet high. Mom and I watched as a neighbor-woman approached him and said, "Mr. Webb, isn't it awful. My poor husband in New York has been hit by a car and is in awful condition in the hospital."

"Then what are you doing here?"

"I can't leave my mother."

"Take her with you."

"Mother can't stand the cold, and she is too old to leave alone."

"If you can't leave your mother you should never have gotten married."

"But the doctor said mother might not last in the cold weather."

"Why don't you take your mother to Alaska, and then maybe you can go to your husband in New York where you belong!"

Dad walked in the house, "Damn fool woman."

I enjoyed a week's visit then flew home. I phoned weekly and received one more letter that winter:

March 10, 1963

I called Mary Lou (granddaughter). Like all young couples it takes time to get on their feet. As my mother used to tell us boys...to get on your feet you first must get off your ass.

We have lots of fruit and grapefruit juice is wonderful, only a dollar per gallon. I am so full of juice I hate to pass a fire hydrant.

We are well. Your mother always liked living in Florida. I like to move about. We expect to be home April 13th. I am starting a job in New Jersey May 6th. Your mother is going with me as the owner will give us a furnished guest house to live in.

Being happy with what you have makes life easier.

The Webbs returned to Williamsburg in time to enjoy the dogwood, get some rest, and prepare for the job in Hopewell, New Jersey. When the work was completed, they returned to Webb's Acre. I received another letter:

June 5, 1963

Your mother informs me I owe $25.00 for dresses. I thought I had outgrown dresses.

We had a pleasant two weeks at Mr. Chorley's farm in Hopewell. They were most kind to us. They stocked up the refrigerator, and we had a lovely bedroom, kitchen, and bath to ourselves. Mr. Chorley called me this morning and wants me to come back in two weeks.

I am decorating their kitchen in old pine and English delph, grapes, and vines. I also selected colors for the West Minister Chapel in Princeton and a Presbyterian Church.

Please be careful driving. On the way home, I was pinched in Maryland, and they took me to jail. Your mother sat in the car waiting.

I got by for $17.50. The state trooper chased me for some distance at 78 miles per hour in a 50 mile zone. The judge said due to my age and LAME leg he would be lenient but to take it easy.

I am working here Thursday and Friday restoring for Colonial Williamsburg. It is some art work that was damaged in transit.

I have decided to stay in Williamsburg for the summer. I am going to do over the interior in a clean and simple way and dispose of a lot of things we never use so there will be less to take care of.

Life on Webb's Acre

During the Restoration years of Williamsburg, Dad's creative talents overflowed. He was a contented artist living on Webb's Acre off of Jamestown Road in a home he built from a drawing sketched on a piece of note paper.

Building, with the help of fellow tradesmen and Shorty, was done on week-ends, holidays, and evenings.

The first construction was a one-car garage that could protect his work tools from weather. Then came their home.

Two bedrooms, one bath, a large living room with a beamed cathedral ceiling, and a narrow stairway leading to a balcony at one end and an oversized fireplace on the opposite side. The kitchen opened onto a porch.

Shortly after moving in Mom said, "I miss having a dining room."

Dad said, "Hell, Rosa, I can fix that." The kitchen became the dining room, the porch became the kitchen.

The next project was a studio with a small fireplace and a large skylight facing north. This was built on the right side of the acre behind the house. Mom said, "I wish you would paint in the house, it gets lonesome in here when you're out there."

"No problem, Rosa." The one-room studio was transformed into a small apartment and rented before the paint was dry.

In their home, Dad removed a window from the larger of the two bedrooms, installed a door, built four steps down to ground level, and a new room with a northern skylight became the studio. It worked fine, until Mom quietly said, "Bob, I miss my porch."

"No problem, Rosa."

A window was removed from the back wall of his studio, a door was added, and what had been a cemented flagstone patio became the floor for the new, screened porch.

Dad and Shorty built a small cottage in the far, right-hand corner of Webb's Acre. While construction was going on, his visiting young grandson asked, "Grandpa, do you have a building permit?"

He and Shorty laughed and hammered away. Blueprints? Permit? It didn't seem right to live in Williamsburg and not have a smokehouse–so up one went! You can't have a smokehouse without a pig to smoke, so a pen was built, and a cute piglet named Colonel arrived. The visiting grandkids fed and watched Colonel grow from a piglet to a fun piggy to a fat hog ready for slaughter.

I asked Dad, "Where did the name come from?"

"I knew a Colonel during the war, he was a son-of-a-bitch. When it comes time to butcher, I'll enjoy it."

Colonel was loved, petted, butchered, and smoked. And for years after Colonel had been consumed, the grandkids asked Gramps when he cooked bacon for breakfast, "Is this Colonel?" He'd grin, "Sure as hell is."

The studio attached to the home wasn't large enough to accommodate some of Dad's art projects. At least, that was the excuse given for building the red barn behind the garage on the left side of Webb's Acre. After a couple of winters, "the Barn" was converted into a one-bedroom apartment and never lacked for a tenant. Later, a screened porch was added.

The rentals, which were fully furnished, offered charm, quietness, beauty, and no lease. The landlord gave verbal restrictions:

No pets, no kids, no parties, and he'd have a key and the right to go into the home whenever he wanted. "And it better damn well be clean or out you go!"

One spring when the Webbs returned from Florida, the young couple in the Cottage had adopted a puppy. The wife pleaded and begged. Between each emotional performance Dad said, "You knew what the rules were. It's either the dog out or you're out. Take your choice." They left.

Bruce Marquardt, a carpenter for the Restoration said, "I had lived in Williamsburg for six months. I met Bob Webb when my wife, Martha, and I went to his house looking for an apartment.

"And who should come around the corner of the smokehouse was none other than *the* Mr. Webb. He asked me, 'What in the hell do you want here?'

"I understand you might have a shack to rent.

"He laughed, and we had an instant friendship.

"We rented 'the Barn.' One time my wife went out of town for the weekend. And with me gone during the day, Bob let himself into "the Barn" and hung a pair of nylon stockings in the shower stall and a size-46 bra on a towel rod so my wife would find them.

"One night he invited my wife and me over for a supper he had made. It was summer, and a fly in the house was also hungry. Mr. Webb caught it in mid-air with his hand and proceeded to kill it by pressing it between his thumb and finger. He placed the dead fly on the edge of his plate and kept right on eating.

"Rosa said, 'Oh Bob, you don't have to do that.'

"He said, 'What's the matter? It ain't bothering nobody now.'

"One time he kept walking in and out of the studio while he was painting a picture of a bushel of apples and a bottle of wine for me. The bottle was sort of cockeyed. I think he was too."

Shorty

Dad had a way of tagging a name to people that described them in appearance or personality. Shorty was thin and slight of build, slow but steady in movement, and shorter than average in height. He was not an ordinary man. He was a giant in what makes a person invaluable to family and friends.

Shorty was a vital part of the never-ending projects on Webb's Acre. He had the gift of knowing how to enjoy his work. He also knew how to tolerate, understand, and cope with a man who could be difficult, kind, generous, and impossible, all at the same time. They shared a unique bond that lasted 48 years.

It was a hot, humid, summer day when Shorty and Dad were digging a ditch for a water pipe. Both were sweating and flinging dirt. Dad said, "Christ, Shorty, you stink!"

Shorty didn't miss a flip of the shovel as he answered with his always-present respect, "Mr. Webb, you don't smell like a rose yourself."

Dad stayed busy working for the Restoration, doing odd jobs and painting pictures. Mom, with the pace her Parkinson's permitted, did the laundry, some cooking, and washing dishes. Virginia, the wonderful black lady, came once a week to do general cleaning. Friends dropped in for visits and left with homemade bread, baked beans, and sliced bacon from the smokehouse.

The Bad Break

One summer day, after Dad had his morning ounces of prevention, he opened the kitchen door, slipped and fell down the steps, and landed with a badly broken right arm.

When the rescue squad arrived and realized who their casualty was, they offered to take him to the hospital if he would buy them a new ambulance. Dad at 5' 10", with a waist line of 54 inches and weighing well over two hundred pounds was no easy task for any rescue squad!

They wheeled him into the emergency room and the attending physician said, "Mr. Webb, I'll give you a shot for pain then set your arm."

He held his arm in midair, "I've already had my shot. Just set the bloody thing."

He endured the itchy cast a little over a week then returned to the doctor, "If the break is in my wrist, why the hell did you put a cast up to my shoulder? Get it off to below the elbow."

The doctor refused.

Shorty was more co-operative and chiseled the cast to below the elbow.

A few days later Dad was raving about the itching under the cast and called his buddy, Shorty, "Get the hammer and chisel and cut this cast lengthwise on each side so I can take the bloody thing off and have a bath."

Shorty hacked a path on each side so there was a top and a bottom. Dad had his shower, rubbed his arm with cocoa butter–his own remedy for the itching–then told Shorty, "Place the bottom and top half back on my arm, and I'll hold it while you wrap this ace bandage around it. That'll keep it in place."

He and Shorty did this for a few baths, then Dad said, "Shorty, why the hell do we need the top part. Just put the bottom part on and wrap the ace bandage around my arm."

During the healing period, Dad managed to drive and keep the home front going until...

He phoned me in New Jersey. "Thelma, your mother and I went to vote for sewers yesterday. On the way out I tripped on the bloody curb and broke my goddamn arm again. I fell against your mother on the way down and knocked her down. She's hurt her leg and can't get out of bed. We are in a hell of a mess."

"Dad, I'll come down and help."

His voice was shaky, "We could use a little help."

I arrived in Williamsburg late that night. I found both of them in need of medical help. Mom couldn't get out of bed. Dad had turned to the bottle in his defeat and in hurt pride said, "I'm sorry I called you. I can manage without you. Just go back where you came from."

I ignored his remark, tended to Mom, coaxed Dad to bed, then went to the guest room and wept for two people I loved.

The early morning sun made things brighter. I drove them to the hospital. Dad's arm was badly bruised, not broken. Mom had a slight fracture in her leg and needed to be hospitalized for two weeks.

I shopped for gowns for Mom, sport shirts for Dad, and bought a supply of groceries.

In a few days, Dad had life back in his control, "You've spent all my money so you might as well leave. I can take care of my own affairs."

I learned as a child to follow his orders. I left.

The outcome of Dad's arm gave him proof that, "Doctors are no goddamn good. Look at my arm if you don't believe me." Then he'd hold the arm up, "See how crooked my wrist is? And I have to live with this crooked wrist for the rest of my life!"

Grandpa Webb

Sherry, at age 12, said, "Mom, I feel sorry for the kids who don't have Grandpa for a grandfather, but I wouldn't want him for a father."

The grandkids knew where their summer vacation would be...Webb's Acre.

The Canaries Arrive

Hannah put her three young daughters on a direct flight from their Oklahoma home to Richmond, Virginia. She had made bright yellow dresses for the girls so they could be easily identified by the Webbs.

Gramps said, "My God, they look like canaries."

Gramps and Gram drove the chirping canaries to Williamsburg. Things went well until the day before they were to fly back to Oklahoma.

Gramps sensed boredom, something not allowed. "Girls, I'm going to show you how they make wine in the old country."

The girls followed him to the garage where he lifted the old galvanized wash tub from its hook. The girls grabbed the handles, and Gramps led them to the back of the property and showed them how to pick ripened, concord grapes.

The four of them lugged the tub back to the house. Gramps sat on the picnic bench, placed his hands on his knees and said, "Okay, girls, this is how they make wine in the old country. Take off your shoes."

He patiently waited for the excited little girls to remove their shoes, then directed, "Now step in the tub carefully and walk around in a circle and squash the grapes."

Squeals of laughter filled the backyard as they formed a merry-go-round to squash the grapes; the juice got knee high. Gram came to the back door, "Oh for heaven's sake Bob! Look at them!"

"Yeah, they're having a hell of a time."

The next day three excited girls were dressed in their canary dresses with their purple legs and Gramps put them on the plane to fly back to their unsuspecting mother in Oklahoma.

New Shoes for All

That was the last summer the flock of canaries flew alone to visit Grandma and Grandpa. The next summer they were chaperoned by their mother.

I drove my three kids down from Richmond so the cousins could have a day of fun together.

Gramps decided they should all have new shoes for school. He, with me and all six kids, went to Casey's, the only department store in town. Each was fitted with saddle backs.

Gramps was getting a kick out of this expedition until it was time to pay the bill. He produced a scene of complaining that has never been forgotten, but was ignored by the salesman, the six kids, and me. His reputation of not wanting to part with a dollar was well known!

I lined up the kids with Gramps to take a picture of this big, never-to-be-forgotten expenditure.

A Sock and a Barrel of Money

Gramps never spent coins, they were for the barrel. The day's collection from purchases went into the toe of a cut-off sock, twisted and placed in his pocket to prevent loose change from wearing a hole in his pants.

The sock became a game second to none. Whenever the grandkids asked to see it, Gramps ceremoniously brought forth the sock, opened it ever so slowly and looked inside. He'd hold it just high enough so the grandchild had to tippy-toe to fish out a coin, usually choosing a nickel because it felt bigger. Occasionally, little fingers found a quarter!

As the kids learned that value sometimes comes in a smaller size, Gramps would go into his act of being poor and begin searching with his fingers through the sock to check for quarters and dimes as the kids jumped and yelled in protest.

A Barrel of Money

When everyone was tucked in bed, all ears could hear the coins click as they dropped into the barrel. Problem was, nobody could find the barrel. The mystery of it was endured for years. With Gramps' encouragement, hours were spent searching, not only in the house, but under the house. Even the adults did some subtle searching, all to no avail.

Typical of Gramps, he had his own unique way to handle life's joys and tragedies. When my family and I were trying to cope with the death of our two-year-old son, Jimmy, Gramps said, "I think it's time to bring out the barrel."

He got a hammer from the garage and went inside the closet under the stairs in the living room. [The stairs led to a small balcony bedroom.] He pulled nails from a false wall that was backed up to the steps. And there, in all its glory, stood the wooden, nail keg.

After Gramps rolled the barrel into the living room, he walked five steps up and pointed to a tiny slot where the step and rise join. The invisible slot allowed coins to drop directly into the hidden barrel. It was easy to see how Gramps was never caught in the act because he was innocently going up or down the stairs.

The family gathered at the old, oak dining table and for several evenings sorted coins. We all gave, and frequently changed, our guesses as to what the total would be.

Gramps had preplanned the activity, even to having a supply of wrappers for the coins. Evenings turned from tears to laughter and Grandma was able to have a new, much-needed refrigerator.

Cream in the Face

The summer Mary Lou and Sherry were visiting together, Gramps was hamming it up with a demonstration of how he'd act when he got old. Whipped cream in aerosol cans had just been introduced to the market and in his old-man posture, he was following the instructions to "shake well." Accidentally, he pressed the release button and whipped cream hit the ceiling. Startled, he looked up to the ceiling and, to the delight of the kids, the glob of whipped cream dropped directly in his face.

The same summer instant potatoes became available. Of course, Grampa had to try them with Mary Lou, Sherry, and Grandma observing the demonstration. He lifted the electric beater from the bowl before turning it off and showered Gram with potatoes. Gram responded, "Oh, Bob."

"How are they Rosa? Are they any good?"

The Wrong Plane

Mary Lou recalls the following unnerving incident:

"Grandpa flew to New Jersey to take me back to Williamsburg. I was too young to fly alone but old enough to remember what happened. It was traumatic!

"Mom drove us to the Newark airport. Gramps had too much to drink and was holding a paper bag full of assorted cheeses not available in Virginia. As we entered the terminal, two airlines were announcing their final boarding messages. We ran and boarded the nearest plane. We were in the air when the Captain announced we would be landing at Columbus, Ohio.

"Gramps hollered, 'I want to go to Patrick Henry Airport in Newport News, Virginia. Why the hell is this plane going to Columbus?'

"Gramps stood up demanding an answer. The paper bag holding his cheese split, the ball of Parmesan dropped to the floor, and rolled down the isle. The Limburger broke open when it hit the floor.

"All I remember is the passengers complaining about the smell, Gramps demanding to be taken to Patrick Henry, and the plane making a special landing someplace. We were put on a plane that flew us to Richmond, Virginia. When we arrived there, we were led to a small plane which landed at Patrick Henry. Grandma and some friends were waiting for us.

"Grandma said, 'Bob, you were supposed to be here a long time ago...'"

Dad rebutted, "Rosa, don't ask...it was a hell of a trip. The airlines don't know what the hell they're doing!"

As Sherry said, "Mom, I feel sorry for the kids who don't have Gramps for a grandfather."

The Great Grandchild

Mary Lou married in her late teens. She and her husband were renting the studio apartment on Webb's Acre, and she was expecting their first baby.

When she went into labor, Gramps insisted upon driving them to the hospital, "I know the short cut on the back roads."

Gram refused to wait at home. "I'm going. I'll sit in the car and wait."

In Dad's haste he missed a turn and compensated for loss of time by turning the headlights on and blowing the horn continuously.

Mary Lou was taken immediately to the labor room. The expectant father and grandfather paced in the waiting room. Gram sat patiently in the car until she became concerned about the long wait and decided to go in the hospital to check on the situation. She opened the car door, lost her balance, and fell. A passerby carried her into the emergency room. Dad was called over the loud speaker, "Mr. Robert Webb, come to emergency immediately."

He raced back and forth from the emergency room for Gram to the maternity ward for Mary Lou.

Finally, the new, unwashed baby was held up in the nursery window to be seen by the anxious first-time father and great-grandfather. Neither had ever seen an unwashed newborn and responded with shocked silence that was broken when Great-grandpa pointed to a rosy-cheeked baby in the nursery, "Do you suppose we could trade it for that one over there?"

Gramps rushed back to emergency to inform Gram they had a great-grandson.

Gram was badly shaken, her glasses broken, her knees scraped, but she was able to leave. Dad placed his arms around her for support, "Rosa, this has been a hell of a night. Let's go home."

The Speed Demon

Gramps' speed limit was never determined by safety. Sherry missed a two-week trip to Nova Scotia with Dad and Mom because I refused to let her ride with the Speed Demon.

Dad phoned upon their return, "Thought you might like to know we are still alive."

Mary Lou and her husband, John, were drinking iced tea at the picnic table and chatting with Gram and me. Dad let the kitchen door bang as he walked toward us. "I'm going to town to get some beer. Anybody wanna go?"

In unison the family answered, "No thanks."

Dad directed a personal invitation to John, "John, how about you? Wanna take a ride?"

"Sure Gramps."

When they returned, Dad was wearing a smile of conquest.

John, with an expression of shock and disbelief, proceeded to tell a story that surprised no one. "On the way back we stopped at a red light, and a police car pulled to my side. I told Gramps, 'There's a police car beside us.' He didn't say anything so I told him again, louder, 'There's a police car on my side.'"

John inhaled deeply and continued, "He made no sign of hearing me, and when the light turned green he shot forward like a bat leaving hell. I yelled, 'Gramps, I told you there was a police car beside us!'"

The tea-sipping audience waited in silence for the Demon Driver to make his statement. "I heard you the first time. The best thing to do is to get to hell out of their way."

The Birthday Present

One day Dad was pulled over for speeding and sadly said to the cop, "This isn't much of a present for my birthday."

The officer was buying into the story until Mom said, "No, Bob, yesterday was your birthday."

The policeman looked at sheepish Dad, then at worried Mom. He closed his book. "Happy birthday, and don't drive so fast."

In telling the story Dad always ended, "...the cop felt sorry for me."

Mom never neglected to add, "Bob, I was afraid he'd notice the birth date on your license."

Life Ends For Mom

My marriage was made in heaven, and I'll take care of Rosa to the end.

The Webbs in Florida–April, 1972

As Dad approached his mid-seventies his tolerance for Mom decreased, his temper worsened, and his drinking increased. As all this was happening to Dad, Mom required more care. In addition to a worsening of the Parkinson's disease, her fits of distrust and jealousy became unbearable.

For ten years, Hannah and I tried to coax Dad into placing Mom in a nursing home. The family doctor lectured many times, "Bob, you have been saving all your life to make sure Rosa was taken care of. Both of you are in a state of emergency. It's time."

Dad used the same five words whenever someone broached this subject, "I can't, and she won't."

Dad had been a care-giver for nearly fifty years. "My marriage was made in heaven, and I'll take care of Rosa to the end."

And God help anyone who dared to interfere.

But now they needed a separation. These two devoted people whose love was unique and beyond understanding were now destroying each other.

Even in the heartbreakingly impossible, there is humor.

Dad, Mom, and I were sitting at the round, oak table having supper. Dad in the captain's chair with his hands folded and resting on his fat belly. Mom sat opposite in a chair Dad had sawed the back off to half its height to make it easier for Mom to sit and stand. Mom's large, brown eyes looked at me, "Your father has a girl friend."

"Mom, what's her name?"

"That's none of your business."

I tried another approach. "Mom, how do you know he has a girl friend?"

"Because he hasn't had anything to do with me for over a year."

I glanced at Dad, a devilish smile on his face, hands still folded, waiting patiently.

"Mom, look at him. He's old. He's fat. He has a tooth missing. Who would want him?"

Mom glared at me, "Plenty of women would want him!"

My attention turned to Dad, who grinned. "Your mother thinks I'm desirable."

I burst into laughter. No way could a third party win against these two characters who had melded into one.

I knew Mom's jealousy had always been a part of their marriage, but as a child I didn't understand. Now I was Bob Webb's grown daughter with an impossible mission to accomplish.

I came with the knowledge that the only way they could survive was to relieve Dad of Mom's care. He could do no more.

Without discussing the subject, I stated I was taking Mom back to New Jersey for a visit. Neither argued.

As I packed Mom's clothes, I recalled Dad's words, "I can't, and she won't."

I wept, "God help me. I have to..."

Caring for Mom

Dad drove Mom and me to the airport. He wept, "I can't take it any longer."

"I know, Dad, I know. I'll phone you in the morning."

I phoned Dad to discuss the nursing home I found about a mile from my apartment. "Dad, there are only two openings. Shouldn't we try it for awhile to give you a rest?"

A moment of silence, then, "We'll try for three months if you get your mother to agree."

The next morning he phoned, "Bring her back. I'll put her in one down here. Let me talk with her."

That's an old story. When he's in Virginia, he's going to wait until they are in Florida. When he's in Florida, it's wait until they are in Virginia.

I lied, "Mom's asleep now. She can't talk to you."

Glendale Nursing Home

My friend, Flo, volunteered to help with what we knew would be a difficult mission.

All hell broke loose when the admitting doctor at Glendale began, "Mrs. Webb, let me tell you about our new nursing home."

Mom, who never swore said, "I don't want to hear about your goddamn nursing home! I have a home of my own."

The doctor signed the papers, and the nurse asked for seventy dollars. Mom yelled, "What the hell did he do for seventy dollars?"

"Mother, you didn't hear correctly. She said seven dollars." As I wrote a check for seventy.

"Your father is trying to get rid of me so he can marry that woman. I won't let her move into my house."

We parked in front of Glendale. The woman in charge approached and invited Mom to see their nice home.

"I don't want to see your home, and I am not going in."

I decided to pull out all the stops. "Mom, you are totally selfish. You never thought of anyone but yourself, and Dad is worn out giving you your way."

Mom glared at me, "You can leave me, and I don't ever want to see you again."

I grabbed my purse and left. Flo stayed to supply Mom with tissues and hear about how mean her younger daughter is, "Bob wasn't able to put me in a home. How come she can?"

Dad didn't know Mom was in Glendale. I was waiting for him to receive my letter reminding him that he had said Mom could stay three months if Mom agreed.

I answered my phone. "Thelma, I got your letter." Then, in a broken voice, "You did the right thing. You have my approval. I can't do anymore. Send Hannah a copy of your letter and attach a note telling her I approve and am satisfied with the arrangement. I'll fly up in a few weeks to visit."

I arrived at Glendale and learned that Mom had fallen three times and needed to be taken to the hospital for x-rays. Two hours later Mom said, "Tell the doctor I'm tired of waiting. If he doesn't come, I'm leaving. There's a Chinese restaurant in Williamsburg. If it doesn't cost too much, we'll eat supper there."

"Mom, you aren't in Virginia."

"Where am I?"

"New Jersey."

"Shit."

"MOTHER!"

"If we aren't back in time for supper, somebody will eat my dessert."

"How do you know?"

"Because a woman didn't go for lunch today, and I ate her dessert. Sponge cake. It was very good."

Mom returned to Glendale in time for supper and all the desserts she wanted.

Mom fell three more times. I wondered how many times in a day Dad had lifted her after falling.

Glendale, unable to locate me, phoned my emergency contact, Muriel, a neighbor. "We cannot handle Mrs. Webb and want her out immediately."

A nursing home has the legal right to place a patient in a taxi and deliver her to the home of the responsible person, but they must first make direct contact with the responsible person.

Muriel located me, "Don't answer your phone and find another home quickly. Your friends and I will relay visits to check on Rosa."

Maplewood

Mom left Glendale with great joy. When the car stopped in front of Maplewood she exclaimed, "This is another goddamn nursing home, and I am not going in!"

A buxom nurse observed the situation and lifted Mom from the car seat. Very gently, she placed Mom in a wheelchair and rolled her into the home.

Mom's new roommate approached and in a soft, gentle voice said "My name is Mary, and I am 84 years old."

I smiled, "Oh, Mary, I don't believe you are 84! You look much younger."

Mom, in a nasty tone said, "That's a goddamn lie. She looks every bit of 84."

Dad Arrives

The phone was ringing when I arrived home. It was Dad, much closer to drunk than sober. "I called Glenwood to talk with your mother, and they told me they couldn't handle her so she left. I want facts! Goddamn facts right now!"

I gave him the straight facts, and every two hours for the rest of the night he phoned giving additional orders, all centered around the plane that I was to put Mom on to send her home in the morning. His last call instructed, "Floyd Martin and I are flying up Friday and leaving Sunday."

I waited at the airport with a wheelchair. Dad walked slowly, "Jesus Christ, don't tell me I've reached that stage!"

Floyd patted the seat, "I'll ride in it, and you can push me."

Visiting Mom was heartbreaking, not for her sake, but for Dad's. Mom was in no pain. Dad was. He examined her body for bruises. He checked the bathroom for a handrail and gave the fixtures a white glove inspection. "This is a nice place."

On Sundays, Maplewood is short on help. Muriel and I went early in the morning to change Mom's bed sheets, clean the bathroom, polish the fixtures, give Mom a bath, put a bright dress on her, and brush her hair. We even washed spots off the floor. Then we fulfilled the mission Dad had sent us on...buying six, red roses.

"It took you a hell of a long time to find them." He held the roses close and started to cry, "They're beautiful. Rosa will like them."

Mom was waiting in a wheelchair in the reception room. She knew Dad; no one else.

He wiped tears, blew his nose, kissed her, and held her hand. "Rosa, what do you want for Christmas?"

"New teeth." [Her gums had shrunk, and the dentures were loose.]

"We love you without teeth."

"No. I want my teeth before Christmas. I'll think of something else for Christmas."

Dad laughed, "Ma, you look all right without them."

"I look like a chicken's asshole without them!"

Through tears and laughter Dad said, "Is that before or after the egg is laid?"

Mom was noticeably tired and was returned to her bed. Dad leaned to kiss her and she said, "I want to go home."

He whispered, "Tomorrow, tomorrow..."

He managed to reach the bench outside the front door, then broke completely. "You see to it your mother has fresh roses and anything else she wants. I can't do anymore. I can't do anymore."

Dad hugged me at the airport, "Your mother is better off close to you. She wouldn't have as much attention in Virginia, and I know I'd go and take her out at one time or another. Maplewood is a nice place—so clean, even clean sheets on Sunday!"

The Hospital

Each day brought a noticeable change for the worse. When I insisted Mom be transferred to a hospital, I phoned Floyd and asked him to talk with Dad.

Dad phoned in the evening. He asked nothing, but said, "You know what to do when you have to."

"Yes, Dad, I will."

On his visit, Dad had confided in me, "Your mother and I have talked about this, and we want to be cremated when the time comes. We want the ashes saved until we are both gone. Then we want the ashes put together in the rose garden under the dining room window. What do you think of that?"

"If that's what you and Mom want, then that's what should be. It doesn't matter what I think, or what anyone else thinks."

He nodded, "Thank you."

He broke the silence, "Thelma, go and make the arrangements now, while I'm here."

I did from my bedroom phone, then I returned to the living room. Dad looked at me, "Did you take care of everything?"

"Yes."

Now we could only wait.

Dad returned to Williamsburg and phoned in the early morning, "I can't go up. I can't get involved anymore. Please take care of it."

"All right, Dad. I will."

Dad phoned every day. Twice he said, "No tube feeding." Another time he said, "Make sure you keep roses–fresh roses–there all the time."

"Dad, we do." Once I asked her if she knew where the roses came from. "Of course–Bob."

Mom was very weak. I asked her, "Do you know who I am?"

"Thelma."

I put my arms around her and began to weep. In a whisper Mom said, "Stop that crying. I have to go sometime."

Courage came to stop the tears, "Mom, do you remember when Hannah's kids squished the grapes and got purple feet?" Mom's smile showed she was understanding and enjoying the memory.

"Do you remember how Dad put boots in front of my bedroom door when I was dating? I'd fall over them, and you and he would know what time I got home? You married quite a character!" Mom's smile broadened, then she was asleep.

I knew it was going to be a race between Mom and Dad, who was driving from Williamsburg with Hannah and Russell. I prayed, "Please God, let her be with you before Dad arrives. He's had enough."

Mary Lou arrived, sat beside the bed, and held Mom's hand. I placed my hand over Gram's heart and rested her head next to mine. The labored breathing stopped...so gradual, so peaceful, then her heart stopped.

"Mary Lou, Grandma's gone. Go and get a nurse."

I held my arm toward Flo, who had been standing quietly in the background. She said, "Three o'clock."

The nurse merely drew the curtains and removed the oxygen and left.

The doctor came and asked me to step into the hall. "Are you all right? We never had this happen before. Usually we have time to try.... I want you to know your mother died of natural causes. There was absolutely nothing we could find to treat. Are you sure you're all right?"

"Doctor, these tears don't mean I am not all right. Do you know this is the first time in my life I have seen my mother when she wasn't shaking from the goddamn Parkinson's? Can you imagine how wonderful she must feel being free from her body? I am all right because I know my mother is at peace now. Please, may she stay in her bed until after my father arrives? He's on the way now."

"Because he's on the way, yes, she may stay."

Dad, Hannah, and Russell arrived within the next 30 minutes. I met them at the main door. Hannah ran to Gram's room. I offered Dad a wheelchair. With a swoop of his cane, he shoved it aside. "I'll walk."

There were no words, no tears, only strength. It was a long walk, but he stood tall and he walked!

In Mom's room, Flo eased him into a wheelchair. The nurse pushed him behind the curtain to be alone with his Rosa. All he said was, "I'm sorry, my dear, so very sorry."

Dad was ready to leave. Mary Lou, Hannah, and Russell drove Dad to the apartment. I spent some time alone with Gram. Then left for my apartment.

I knew my apartment would be full of people when I arrived, and I had yet to call the funeral home. I closed my bedroom door to do so and felt relieved that arrangements had been previously made.

With that taken care of, I returned to the living room. Dad was conversing with each friend, "This is a crazy house. People are coming and going all the time as though they live here."

Then he said, "We stopped for gas on the way up, and I looked at my watch. It was exactly three o'clock. I told Hannah and Russell, Grandma's gone. She's gone. We don't need to rush."

My eyes met Flo's. It was three o'clock when she held her arm up.

It was October 22, 1974.

Mom Goes Home

All is not finished.

Hannah and Russell returned to their Oklahoma home. Dad was alone in Williamsburg, and Mom's ashes were in the New Jersey funeral home. Dad wanted the ashes in Williamsburg.

I contacted the funeral home and asked how that could be arranged. "No problem. We ship them parcel post whenever you request us to."

Send my mother parcel post through the U.S. mail? Have Dad walk to the end of the drive and take her out of the mailbox? My God, how barbaric! No! Never! Somehow I'll do it myself.

I made arrangements with the funeral home to hold the ashes for personal pick-up the next day.

I arrived five minutes before the business office closed and walked down the vacant hall. It was a weird feeling.

A man in a dark suit approached, "May I help you?"

I handed him a Macy's shopping bag, "I have come for the package."

The man reached for the shopping bag, "What package?"

"Mrs. Webb."

He disappeared, reappeared and handed me the Macy shopping bag, which now held a box. As I reached to accept the shopping bag, he released his hold. The unexpected weight caused my arm to drop.

I opened the car trunk and tucked the package way in the back in a secure spot. I was unable to speak or cry...nothing, except to perform the physical motion of what had to be done.

My friend Bette had accepted the invitation to visit Webb's Acre. When our luggage was in the trunk we headed for Williamsburg. Bette said, "Thelma, you've had a rough few months. Why don't you let me drive? You relax."

"Thanks, I'm okay. If I get tired, I'll let you know."

I thought, "God, you and I are the only ones who know where mother is. Please don't let there be an accident."

It was dusk when we arrived at Webb's Acre and unloaded the suitcases. Bette pointed to the shopping bag in the far back, "I can carry that."

I closed the trunk, "I'll do that in the morning."

Bette's large, blue eyes glared, "That's your mother!"

"I'll take care of it in the morning."

"My God, I wouldn't have come had I known…"

Dad opened the kitchen screen, "Where the hell have you been? Supper's been in the oven for hours."

He was doing great. A fire in the fireplace, his homemade bread, and his Boston baked beans for supper.

We awakened to the smell of home-cured ham frying, fresh bread being toasted, and scrambled eggs. He had a towel tucked in his pants for an apron, "Can't resist good eating, huh?"

After breakfast I said, "Dad, let's go to your studio."

Bette cleared the table, and I followed Dad to the studio. "I know why you're here. You brought your mother home. You wouldn't let me go to the mailbox…I'll show you where to put…"

He led me into the dining room and opened the little door in the left end of the side-board. He removed a few items, then pointed with his cane, "In there." He walked away saying, "Take care of it later."

Later came when we returned from a visit to Williamsburg Pottery, which Dad described as "a hell of a mess."

I said, "Bette, go in and tell him I want to take care of the package now and keep him company."

I carried the shopping bag through the kitchen to the dining room and whispered, "Well, Mom, I took you away, now I'm bringing you home." I folded the shopping bag to fit in the opening, then closed the door. I felt relieved that my last chore was completed.

It wasn't.

Dad handed me a pen and paper, then dictated a message, "The contents of the package is the remains of Grandmother Webb. Please do not disturb." He handed me cellophane tape, "Put it on the inside of the door."

He disappeared, returned with a hammer and one nail…the door was secured.

While Bette and I went to Carter's Grove, Dad chose to stay home and cook supper: black-eyed peas and chunks of ham simmered in the large, iron pot hanging from the crane in the oversize fireplace. And more home-baked bread!

Bette and I left Webb's Acre loaded with seven loaves of bread, a pot of home-baked beans, a jug of wine cider, and a slab of home-cured bacon. He was his old happy self, fussing, "You're taking a hell of a lot more than you came with."

The same complaints he expressed when he received the assorted tubes of oils and paint brushes from his New Jersey friends, "Yeah, I know, they all want a painting."

As was customary, he stood in the driveway with a handkerchief in each hand and waved good-by. I wept for this man who gave everything for over 50 years without ever receiving a verbal thank you.

I wept for the woman who was so sick she couldn't overcome her inability to give thanks. Perhaps she didn't even know that thanks were due. Perhaps they weren't.

Serving Stew to Bette
from the Fireplace

Life Alone

*Oh, Dad, you are too,
too, too much!*

Dad and Lil by the Card Tree

Dad's New Jersey friends, Lil and Brian, were concerned about his being alone for Christmas, so they sent a card inviting him for the holidays. Several friends phoned. He gave excuses, the last being, "I can't afford it."

Lil responded, "We're taking up a collection to cover your flight."

That did it!

"All right I'll come, but no fuss."

"Okay, Dad, no fuss. We'll go out for dinner, and we won't even have a tree."

"Make sure. No fuss."

I spread the victory news to friends who totally ignored "no fuss."

Brian insisted there certainly would be a tree and found a beauty. He set it in a large flower pot full of sand. He wrapped a rope around the tree, then tied it onto the handle of the sliding glass door. The top was bent to make a snug fit on the ceiling. It stood tall, straight, naked, and covered half of the small living room. I had no ornaments or tinsel. Lil, the creative one, said, "Tape your Christmas cards to the branches as they come in the mail."

A *Friendship tree* was in the making with no fuss, as requested!

I met Dad at the Newark airport, allowing time to locate a wheelchair. When his plane was taxiing into position, I pushed the chair through the double doors and walked quickly down the covered ramp.

Two uniformed men ran up to me. One grabbed the chair, the other my arm. With forced encouragement, they led me back through the double doors yelling, "You can't come down here! You stopped all operations when you came through those doors."

"I'm sorry, but my father needs a wheelchair."

When the plane stopped, one man guided the wheelchair down the ramp, the second man ordered me to stay put.

Dad was in the first group of passengers. I pointed and yelled, "There's a wheelchair for you back there."

He continued to walk at a fast clip, "What's the chair for? You got troubles and want me to push you?"

Mr. Show-off had lost fifteen pounds and looked great.

"I don't know what the hell happened. All of a sudden, the plane stopped and all the lights went out–everything just stopped!"

I played ignorant, "Probably some slight electrical problem."

We weren't in the apartment ten minutes before friends arrived to welcome Dad. He loved the tree and assigned himself the job of taping Christmas cards on as they came in.

I gave him my bed, and I slept on a foam mattress on the floor. In the morning he said, "I couldn't sleep all night knowing you were on the floor. Why don't you sleep on the sofa?"

That night I slept on the lumpy, too-short sofa. In the morning Dad said, "You look tired."

"I slept on the sofa to make you happy. Sleeping on the floor would have provided me a night's sleep."

"Then why the hell don't you sleep on the floor?"

Christmas Eve

On Christmas Eve, Dad wanted to watch *A Christmas Carol* on television. The story of Ebenezer Scrooge had two things going for Dad: it is in color and it is based in England. Dad believed anything English was bigger and better, unless he was in an anti-English mood. Then it was "those bloody English."

My date arrived at the beginning of the television show and insisted I go to his home to see his tree. On my return, an hour later, my date handed me a gift with instructions not to open it until the next day.

"Dad, I'm sorry I left you alone."

"Thelm, the more alone we are, the closer we are to the true meaning of Christmas."

I couldn't respond.

Dad broke the silence. "Let's see what's in the box."

We ripped open the package, and within was an exquisite, white, see-through negligee set. My reaction was disbelief. Dad's was a hearty laugh that lasted till bedtime.

Lil came for Christmas breakfast with a loaf of her homemade bread. On the first bite, Dad said, "God, I'm never going to bake another loaf of bread! This is wonderful!"

Muriel arrived with a frozen bluefish–it was huge! Lil and I wrapped it well in aluminum foil: head, tail, all of it. A wide, red ribbon was tied around the neck. We painted large eyes with gorgeous lashes on each side of the head. Then, to complete the masterpiece, a big, smiling mouth.

We placed it in the freezer for Dad to take back to Williamsburg.

Christmas Day Party

Dad and I couldn't find a restaurant open for Christmas dinner. "Don't worry, Dad, I know where there's an open house for widows and widowers who have no place to go for Christmas dinner. And it's free!"

"You're kidding. How can I go? I don't know the people."

"Since when was that a problem for you?"

Harold, a Jewish widower, gave a warm welcome to all his guests, plus a gourmet buffet, a decorated tree, dance music, and a present for each. A young woman pinned a name tag on Dad's lapel, *Bob Webb, Thelma's father*.

It wasn't long before Dad became Bob. One-by-one he charmed each guest with his wit and infectious laugh. At one point he passed me, "These are wonderful people. I'm having fun!"

"Yeah, I can tell!"

To drive home, I chose the road on top of the mountain so Dad could see the lights of New York in the distance–a breathtaking sight.

Quietly Dad said, "You know, Thelma, this is the best Christmas I have ever had in my entire life. Everyone is at peace, even your mother."

Ol' Scrooge at the Supermarket

Dad, who loves to browse in grocery stores, went his way while I shopped. As I waited in the checkout line, I noticed Dad by the gum machine with a stocking-capped kid. Dad's cane hung over his coat sleeve. The little fellow was on tippy-toes helping to find a coin in the toe of the cut-off money sock, just as I had seen my children do many times. I knew by the smiles that they were successful. Two, so far apart in years, smiling at each other in wordless communication. Both unaware of any onlookers until I approached. "Come on, Scrooge, let's go."

Departure

Before we left for the airport, we wrapped the fish in newspaper. This beauty would be presented to Floyd from his New Jersey friends.

Dad sat at the airport, holding the fish. "I don't want to go. I have never had such a wonderful week in my life. I have never met so many kind people. I don't want to leave."

He hugged me and through tears said, "God bless you."

Neither of us realized it would be a matter of only a few weeks before Dad would have to be rescued from an old fool's folly.

Trouble Brews

Floyd drove Dad to Sarasota in January. I phoned the first week and was assured he was able to cope alone.

The second week he answered, "I'm keeping myself busy. I'll survive."

On the next check-up, I offered to fly down to visit.

"No need to. I'm keeping busy."

He sounded better on each call, "You don't have to phone. I'm doing fine."

I waited a few extra days before calling and again offered to visit.

"Hell, I'm busy. You don't need to visit."

Two months of frequent phoning and Dad sounded happier and happier. On the next call, he said, "Why the hell do you keep calling? If I need you I'll let you know, just stay where you are."

That did it. I made flight arrangements and one more phone call to tell him the day and the flight to meet.

The plane landed, and I spotted him in the waiting crowd dressed in a sporty, new jacket, bow tie, a big grin, and a young, beautifully dressed woman standing beside him.

With a welcoming hug he said, "Thelma, this is Janie Moore."

I assumed she was a kind neighbor driving Dad to the airport. We settled into the Grandpa-green Chrysler, and Janie automatically sat in the driver's seat.

Dad said, "Janie is going to take us to her house and show you what we've been doing."

The show consisted of a renovation of her two-floor, older home. Custom-made draperies, new carpeting, new kitchen cabinets, with a shiny, new floor. The tour continued on the second floor.

Draperies to match the bedspreads, more new carpet, and a bathroom fit for a magazine cover.

"Dad, I think we better leave. I'll drive."

In the mobile home we sat at the kitchen table, Dad with a beer, me with iced tea. "Well, what do you think of Janie? She's the receptionist for my dentist. She'll go to Williamsburg and be a housekeeper for me. We're all going out for dinner tonight."

"Did she say she was going to Williamsburg?"

"Not yet."

"Dad, you take her out for dinner and ask her point blank what her intentions are. I don't think she plans to go anyplace. I'll stay here."

Dad agreed. I walked around the mobile park and a neighbor approached, "Have you met your father's girl friend yet?"

"Yes, they're out for dinner now."

"I don't mean the dark-haired one. I'm talking about the one with long, blonde hair."

"Blonde hair?"

"Yes, she arrives about ten every night in a red convertible and spends the night."

My mind was still spinning when Dad arrived home from dinner, "Well, you were right. I asked her about going to Williamsburg. She said I should talk to my minister, and he could help me find a housekeeper."

There wasn't time to further the conversation as a red convertible with the top down arrived with a blonde.

She knew her way in, "Hi, Bob. You must be Thelma." In her next breath, she said, "I keep telling your father Janie Moore is a gold digger. She has a boyfriend that comes right after your father leaves, and he spends nights with her. Bob won't believe me."

The blonde was Ursula with a German accent. She worked in a local bar and knew all the gossip. I responded favorably to her honesty and agreed the three of us should ride to Janie's and see for ourselves. The Chrysler was parked across the road from Janie's house, and we sat in the dark, waiting.

Ursula was right...the boyfriend arrived by ten-thirty.

We returned to Dad's. No comments were needed by any one. Blondie and Dad had a few beers, then she removed her high heels and slept on the sofa. Dad retired to his twin bed to sleep, and I crawled on Mom's bed but couldn't sleep. My mind was planning a visit to Janie's dentist the next day.

I walked into the dentist's office and said to the nervous receptionist, "I will stay here until I see the dentist."

The middle-aged dentist became noticeably disturbed as I detailed Janie Moore's relationship with one of his patients.

"I don't like this, and I won't stand to have her use my patients. I wondered where she was getting all the new clothes and jewelry."

"Jewelry?"

That evening I confronted Dad about the jewelry. I concluded, "Get it back from her."

"I'm not an Indian giver."

"Old man, start packing. We leave tomorrow for Williamsburg!"

Blondie arrived at her usual time and helped to load the car, had beer with Dad, flipped her high heels off, and had her last night's sleep on the sofa.

Dad was giving full cooperation and had nothing to say as the Chrysler left the mobile park. I was still in a bad mood, "There's nothing like an old fool making a damn fool of himself."

Dad chuckled, "But I had such a hell of a good time..."

He giggled some more then started side-seat driving, "That light's turning red. Careful, there's a car coming down the side street. Get in the right lane..."

I knew I'd never last three days under his guidance and decided to try diplomacy. "Dad, I've been driving many years and have never had an accident. I'm accustomed to driving alone, and it makes me nervous to have someone directing me."

He twisted his body toward me, placed his hands on his hips and in a sarcastic tone said, "Well, it doesn't take a whole hell of a lot to make you nervous."

Home on Webb's Acre

I stayed in Williamsburg helping Dad settle in. Then he informed me, "You can leave. I'll tend to my own affairs."

A month later I phoned, "Dad, is the dogwood in bloom yet?"

"Not till next week."

"Then I'll wait until next week to come down."

"The dogwood will be here, but I might not be."

"I'll be down tomorrow."

I'm Here-Doing

I drove to Williamsburg to check how Dad was coping with his enforced changes. I realized Dad had lost not only his wife, but also his full-time nursing job. For the first time in his life, he was totally alone. Could he adjust?

As I turned in the driveway, I noticed a beautifully painted sign in the front yard...*For Sale, Inquire Within.*

"Oh, God, is he selling the homestead?"

Dad was sweeping the back patio when I arrived, and I gave him a hug. "Dad, how are you doing?"

"I'm here...doing!"

"Maybe, if you take one day at a time, life will get better."

He leaned on the broom handle, looked straight into my eyes, "My life will be exactly what I make it."

"Well," I thought, "so much for my wisdom!"

I didn't have the courage to ask about the *For Sale* sign.

The next day a young couple knocked on the kitchen door. "We saw the *For Sale* sign..."

"Yeah, come on in, sit down. I'm Bob Webb. Just finished baking bread. Sit down and have some."

He placed sliced bread, sorghum molasses, and beer on the old, round, oak table.

The young fellow said, "This is wonderful. My grandmother used to bake bread."

After dipping several slices of the warm bread in the molasses, he said, "Mr. Webb, we'd like to see the house."

"Go ahead. It's here. Take a look."

Dad sat patiently in his captain's chair while they went on an unguided tour of the house. It was a labor of love built on weekends and evenings by Dad with the help of a plumber, an electrician, and Shorty. The living room has a large, walk-in fireplace and wide boards of pine for flooring. At the end of the living room with a beamed cathedral ceiling is a narrow stairway leading to a small, upstairs balcony bedroom. Throughout there is the warmth and charm of natural wood; oil paintings hang every-where, even in the bathrooms.

Tramp Artist: The Life of Robert Webb

The couple returned in awe to the dining room, "Mr. Webb, how much are you asking for it?"

"How much would you pay? Sit down and we'll talk."

More bread was sliced, more molasses dunked, more beer poured. The spider had trapped his flies. And I realized the old devil was playing a game and had no intention of selling the homestead! The young couple departed in high spirits, with no questions answered.

"Dad, you ought to be ashamed of yourself!"

"We had a hell of a good time, didn't we? They'll be back for more bread and molasses."

That evening, after supper we sat by the fireplace watching the flames. Quietly he said, "When I go to bed, I think of something to do the next morning. It might be nothing except to make a fire in the fireplace, but when I wake up I have something to do and that gets me out of bed. I might not ever get to building the fire, but it gets me going."

Housekeepers Come and Go

Dad's determination to control his life independently did keep him busy. Shorty came regularly to help with outside chores. Floyd and other friends stopped by for chats. In between my frequent visits, events happened that I learned about from outside sources...never from the horse's mouth. Housekeepers came and went, mostly went.

Housekeeper One

Floyd said, "He had one in particular, a German girl, who was just a gold digger, and he put new tires on her car. She was from Florida and had a red convertible.

"I dropped in for a visit. They'd had a big argument. He was back in the studio bedroom, so I talked to him about letting her go. He said, 'Yeah, goddamn it, I'll let you do it.'

"I said, 'I'll get rid of her. Don't worry.' It was night, so I went on out and told her, 'You got to go.'

"She said, 'Where?'

"I don't care where. You just got to get out of this house. I've had orders to get you out. You gotta go.

"She went back to her supper, then said, 'Well, let me go in and tell that old fool good-bye.'

"She went in and said, 'Mr. Webb, I'm leaving. You're just a damned old fool anyway!'

"He said, 'Just get to hell out of here!'

"He had his long drawers on...I'll never forget it. It was comical. But she left that night. I stayed right there until she left."

I laughed, "That was Ursula from the barroom in Sarasota. I didn't know she was here."

Housekeeper Two

Dad had another housekeeper from Florida: Louise. She was quite nice and had two daughters: Cindy, a teenager, and Vicky, who was twenty. He gave them a home and outfitted them with clothes. Referring to Louise, Dad said, "I have good meals, clean clothes, and a clean bed. I consider I am very lucky."

Louise lasted a year. Then he was on his own again.

Dad phoned me that summer and said, "Shorty and I have put your mother in the rose garden today. You'll just have to take care of me when the time comes."

Counting Ursula, Dad had two housekeepers. I happened to be visiting when he was interviewing a prospective third housekeeper.

Dad listened tentatively as the woman talked and talked and talked.

I remained silent, wondering how he was going to conclude the interview. It ended abruptly when he stood up, looked at the woman, and said, "The doctor must have given you a shot with a Victrola needle."

Dad walked out of the house, leaving me with the poor soul who continued to talk.

I placed an arm around the woman's waist and led her, still talking, to her car. She opened the car door, "I don't think you would be happy here. He's very difficult."

I located Dad in the garage, "Couldn't you have been a little kinder?"

"Jesus Christ, who the hell could put up with her mouth? I'll do my own goddamn cooking and cleaning."

"That's a good idea because nobody could put up with you!"

And he did, up to the time Floyd drove him to Sarasota for another winter.

A Short Winter in Sarasota

I prayed that there would be no emergencies this winter.

A few weeks after his departure, I received a phone call.

"It's your old man. I'm back in Williamsburg. Flew in last night."

Panic set in, "What's the matter?"

"Nothing. I sold the mobile home for four thousand and decided I've got food, heat, and a good bed right here. So what the hell do I need to go to Florida for?"

"You what!?"

"Sold everything...furniture, paintings, everything–and walked out. I'm gonna stay right here. So that's that."

I didn't know whether to laugh or cry, but I did know he didn't sell it...he gave it away.

Then Dad offered some good news, "I'm going to start painting."

Mom's illness had demanded more and more of Dad's time, so he hadn't painted for several years. To hear him say he was going to paint again was wonderful. He did spend the winter eating, keeping warm, and painting with renewed energy.

Backyard Show

On a visit in the spring, I suggested we have a private art show in the backyard. We carried the paintings of various sizes outside and leaned some against the house and propped others against chairs and trees. We positioned two chairs to sit in, offering a panoramic view of the display.

What a show!

Dad exclaimed, "My God, I can't believe I painted them!"

I remarked, "Dad, your paintings are brighter in color, more relaxed, and they are so cheerful. They're unbelievable!"

He nodded his head and quietly said, "Your mother has been taken care of. I don't have to worry anymore."

And I thought my worries were over as well...they weren't.

Housekeeper Three

Sometimes as a step toward returning to the real world, patients at the State hospital in Williamsburg are placed in homes as helpers. Dad had such a lady helping him in his home. She was capable, pleasant, and able to enjoy (and survive) Dad's unpredictable personality.

Several months into her job she said, "There's a woman at the hospital who teaches crafts, may I invite her for dinner?"

Dad answered, "I don't give a damn who you invite. Just get the food on the table!"

Within a few weeks, No. 3 was no longer living at Webb's Acre. The invited guest had moved in with her few worldly possessions and became housekeeper No. 4.

Friends and family had mixed feelings about No. 4, but, as with previous housekeepers, no one said anything. Everyone knew better than to interfere with Dad's life. He was in charge...or was he?

Housekeeper Four

I felt a need to visit Dad. He was doing well for a man in his early eighties, but one never knows....

When I arrived from New Jersey, Kathy, Dad's housekeeper of a year, was working in the garden. Dad was sitting on his bench beneath the kitchen window sipping his ounces of prevention. He looked great. I followed him into the dining room where he showed me a miniature ceramic chamber pot Kathy had made. He said, "Isn't that cute?"

He then led me on a tour of the changes Kathy had made in the house: shelves, lights, rearranged furniture, a stove installed in the oversize fireplace for heat and cooking. Kathy had really expressed herself around the house. It was different and interesting.

The tour ended where it began, at the dining-room table. Again, Dad picked up the miniature chamber pot in order to admire Kathy's ceramic skill. Then he said, "Go upstairs, you'll see some more of her work."

Tramp Artist: The Life of Robert Webb

I climbed the narrow stairs at the end of the living room that led into a small open balcony bedroom. Oh my!

A new bedspread, chair, lamp, and bookcase loaded with Kathy's books and a large, full-sized chamber pot...a duplicate of the miniature one–except this one had large letters in gold: R-O-B-E-R-T and K-A-T-H-Y....

I sat in the chair, held the pot in my hand, and turned it carefully to read:

ROBERT AND KATHY WEBB 1978.

I thought, "Dear God, did he send me up here to read on a piss-pot that he is married to Kathy?"

I read it over and over. Numbness ran through my body. Could it be a joke? Or is it true?

With the aid of the handrail, I went down the steep, narrow steps. Dad, sitting in his captain's chair asked, "Did you see her pottery?"

"Yes, she does nice work."

I could say no more and hoped to God that my outward appearance was better than what I was feeling on the inside.

Kathy came in from the garden and greeted me with open arms. We all drove to town for supper, returned to the house, and had a short visit in the living room. Then we retired...each to our own individual room.

I had the feeling I would leave Williamsburg without being able to ask–or without being informed–if a chamber pot was telling me I had a stepmother younger than I.

If it is true...why? Did she insist on marriage for security reasons?

Good God! A chamber pot as a wedding announcement! I don't believe it, but that's a lot of work for a joke, and gold is expensive.

"Oh, Dad, you are too, too, too much!"

The day before leaving, Dad talked with me. "Kathy kept telling me she doesn't come from a family where a woman lives with a man without marriage."

They had separate bedrooms and baths–Dad was nearly 82, Kathy some 30 years younger–why this pressure for marriage after living in his home for over a year?

But they *were* married and later went on a cruise to several countries, including Russia. Upon returning from the journey, Kathy made it difficult for family and friends of many years to maintain a relationship with Dad.

Although Dad's health was noticeably failing, I continued phone calls and visits over the next few years. An excerpt from a letter written to my daughter, Sherry, who was living in Jamaica, expresses some of the stress we were all feeling during this difficult period of his life:

"Grandpa is failing. Losing weight fast. If you can, send him a note and tell him about your kids. Yes, I know 87 is many years, but somehow I feel amputated from my beginning. I selfishly want to know he is touchable."

Life Ends for Dad

Mom and Dad in Their Garden
beneath the Dining-Room Window

On July 10, l986, he drifted away in his own bed.
I love you and was blessed
to have you for my parents.

O n Sunday, July 6, 1986, a Williamsburg neighbor phoned me while I was visiting a friend in Pennsylvania. Dad was in the hospital. I had been with Dad two weeks earlier and knew he would not be with us much longer. At that time, I hugged and kissed him over and over and told him how much I loved him.

I placed the phone back in the receiver and rationalized that there was nothing more I could do–there was no reason for me to return to Williamsburg. All that could be done was being done. I would not go.

The next morning, as I prepared to drive to Williamsburg, I asked myself, "Why? I said my goodbye. Yet here I am on the way... I have to go. Why?"

It was past visiting hours when I walked into the hospital toward his room. I opened his door slowly and saw his thin body turned toward the window. I began to weep. I closed his door and found the waiting room empty. I sat and cried uncontrollably. Two weeks ago, I knew he would not be with me much longer. Now I knew the time had come to face that reality.

I recalled the many times as a child when I'd be crying and Dad would say, "Your bladder is too close to your eyes! Learn to control it."

I got my "bladder" under control and returned to his room. I walked to the far side of his bed.

"Hi, Dad."

Silently he opened his arms, and I leaned into them. He patted my shoulder, and we held each other close for a long time.

In a soft, weak voice, "Thelm, when I raise my arm..."–and he demonstrated–"that means give me a small piece of ice."

"Okay, Dad."

Seconds later in a loud, clear voice, "Well, goddamn it, my arm is up!"

I laughed, "I thought you were just demonstrating."

As I reached for the glass with chipped ice, I heard his voice, "Dummy."

Now I knew we were back on track, and I'd be able to handle whatever was to come. We did little talking. It was mostly the arm signal for ice, which would cause him to cough and spit up the water. It became an endless cycle that exhausted both of us. Finally, after three hours, the signals stopped and he slept. I sat by the bed holding his hand, trying to control my "bladder." When I felt he would sleep for a few hours, I left to find a motel.

I returned the next morning and found an attractive, dark-haired woman following the arm signal for ice. The woman smiled and said, "Hello!"

I responded, "Hi," then realized–for crying out loud–this was my sister, Hannah, whom I hadn't seen in several years!

I went over to hug her, "If I thought I'd look as young as you do, I'd dye my hair."

"I don't dye mine."

A strong voice interrupted, "Cut out the socializing and give me some ice."

Tramp Artist: The Life of Robert Webb

Dad developed additional signals representing other needs he wanted fulfilled. He kept Hannah and me busy full time. A nurse remarked, "He certainly is demanding."

"Yes," I answered, "He's always been demanding, but he demanded as much of himself as he did the rest of us."

I recalled how he cared for our handicapped mother for the 48 years of their marriage, never complaining, but demanding much of everyone, including mother. His demands kept Mom as busy and as active as her body would allow. It kept her alive many years beyond expectations.

Over the next few days his orders changed as his condition worsened. Mostly, he said he just wanted to go home.

I said, "Dad, you haven't closed your eyes for hours."

He whispered, "I'm afraid."

"You want to go home, don't you?"

He nodded his head and made the sign of the cross in the air.

This man knew what was happening, and he knew what he wanted. He never lost his strong personality or direct language. At one point, Dad, in a soft weak voice, said something to Hannah. She asked him to repeat it. A second time she asked him to repeat it. Taking a deep breath he belted out, "If you'd clean the shit out of your ears, you could hear me!"

Arrangements were made for the rescue squad to take him home where a rented hospital bed had been placed adjacent to his bed in the studio bedroom. I explained all this to him and said, "It won't be long now."

He looked directly at me and said. "That's what the rabbi said when he circumcised the baby!"

Once again he had the last word!

I met his doctor one time and that was the morning Dad was to leave the hospital. When I asked what was really happening to Dad, he answered, "I can only guess. He refused to have any testing." Then added, "I hope when my time comes, I can do exactly what he is doing."

Hannah was unable to stay and returned to her home in Florida. Kathy, Dad's wife, remained mostly at home with occasional visits to the hospital.

In the morning, the rescue squad arrived, and Dad was taken home and placed in a hospital bed. After they left, he glanced over at his bed and ordered, "Make my bed."

"Dad, your bed is made, but you are better off in the hospital bed..."

"Put me in my own bed. Now!"

Again, I obeyed. When he was in his bed, he reached up to his nose and removed the oxygen tube.

In less than 24 hours–on July 10, 1986–he drifted away in his own bed.

Afterglow

Could I cry? No! It was only once in the hospital when I was sitting by his bed and thought he was asleep that I began to cry. Like Mom had done, he ordered, "Stop it."

Now there simply was not time. His requests had not been totally fulfilled.

While Dad's body was being cremated, a friend and I were busy weeding the rose garden beneath the dining-room window. This is where Mom's ashes had been placed a year after her death. When the weeding was finished, we positioned potted flowers in the garden and two red roses in a bud vase. Five small American flags outlined the edge of the semi-circle garden. It was beautiful.

Sunday, July 13, 1986, was a warm, sunny day. A few close friends, two grandchildren, and one great-grandchild gathered in the driveway for a service. Using an ice-cream scoop that I had given Mom years ago, I trenched a cross in the ground.

Shorty stepped in the soil beneath the dining room window, bent his knees to a kneeling position, and scratched a circle in the soil with his fingers. "This is where Mr. Webb told me he wanted his ashes. This is where we put Mrs. Webb's ashes."

I pulled rank–now being the oldest generation.

"He's getting a cross because that's what I want."

As I continued trenching the cross, Dad's great-grandchild asked his mother, "What's Grandma doing?"

"Making a place for Grandpa."

I heard my daughter crying. Without interrupting my job of trenching, I ordered, "Stop it!"

To Dad, I said, "You never make anything easy!"

The Eulogy

The service that Dad did not want–but which I did want for Mom, the family, and for him–began in the presence of family, a few friends, Shorty, and Floyd. They stood in the driveway as I read from the notes I had written the previous night:

> When Mother died, Dad told me they both wanted to be cremated. The ashes of whoever died first would rest until the other died. Then their ashes were to be put together on Webb's Acre for eternity. We are here to fulfill their wishes.

> Hannah and I were their only children. We grew up in the environment of what most marriages include. Their marriage of over 50 years went beyond that because of Dad's creative gift and Mother's physical handicap. Their relationship was intense and alive, never dull, and with total devotion to each other.

> Dad had asked Floyd Martin, a special friend, to place his ashes here with Mother's. (Floyd carefully filled the trenched cross with Dad's ashes.)

I requested that my daughter's husband read Psalm 23 and to lead us in the Lord's Prayer.

I continued:

> The five flags represent Dad's devotion to his service in the United States Navy during World War I. They will be given to his five great-grandchildren.

> The potted plants are from family and friends. We would like to have a few left here with Mother and Dad. Please take the others to plant in your home garden in remembrance of them.

> Three months before Mother died, Dad requested that I have a fresh red rose by her bedside each day. I did so.

> Today, we have one red rose for you, Mother, and one red rose for you, Dad.

> We love you and thank you for being part of us.

> I love you and was blessed to have you for my parents.

> God Bless you both.

Tramp Artist: The Life of Robert Webb

Love Letters

*My Dearest,
and Hannah and
Thelma...*

Rosa, Hannah, and
Thelma, 1931

The letters that Dad wrote to my mother while he was away working in Rhode Island appear in this chapter. They provide a personal glimpse of the relationship that existed between a young artist who wrote from his job in Newport to his beautiful, auburn-haired wife who was caring for their two young daughters in Montclair, New Jersey. Because of Mom's failing health, not yet diagnosed as Parkinson's disease, Dad's parents left their home in Florida to help Mom in New Jersey.

These letters were written during a period of five months, January through May of 1931, at the height of the Great Depression. They reveal his loneliness for his family and Mom's growing mistrust, a condition of her yet-to-be diagnosed Parkinson's disease.

Lonely Times

Although Hannah and I were always included in the salutation, the letters were written to Mom.

115 John Street

Newport, R.I.

January 16, 1931

Dearest and Thelma and Hannah,

Well dear, I have been busy getting our stock room ready. Mr. Baum has arrived and I have been busy with him and expect to be Sat–Sun. The boarding house we are in is not so fancy but very good eats. Twelve a week for room and board. The bed is good and clean. I went to a hotel and they asked me seven a day, some difference. Rose dear, I want you to call up Bosch Peatts, the paper company and ask for Mr. Mason. Tell him to send me at once C.O.D. 200 single rolls of lining paper, R. Webb, decorator, Count Villa job Newport, R.I. and don't forget the discount. Tell him I am waiting for it. Thank you dear.

Love the girls for me and lots for yourself my only love, and take care of yourself and pray for me as I do for you. So long, Honey.

xxxx Daddy

[Date unknown, except 1931]

My Dearest and Hannah and Thelma,

Well dear, I just finished with my books. I have plenty to think of along with thinking of you all the time. I miss you so much. I love you more everyday and so glad you feel better. Will write later in the week and tell you what time to leave and I will meet you in Providence and believe me I will be on time to get you in my arms. This is a fine room, ½ size bed but that is plenty big enough for you and me. I get my meals with the rest of them over to the old French woman's. She sure can cook. I know you will like her cooking. Well dear, I have been a good boy as you asked me to and will be the rest of my life just for you, so please don't make me feel as though you can't trust me.

Write often my love. From your Daddy xxx

February 12, 1931

My Dearest and Thelma and Hannah,

Well how are all three of my funny faces getting along? Don't be lonesome because that keeps you from getting better. Of course I love you and no one else. Now you have it in writing but it is alright dear. I got the handkerchiefs today and will look forward for my bathrobe. I sure am working hard enough for a little comfort. You always wishing the job was done. Be reasonable, give me a chance to make a dollar. You should think yourself lucky that I have something to do. Write often, my love, and be a good girl.
From your Daddy xxxx

February 16, 1931

My Dearest,

Received your letter today. I hope you found out from the telephone operator where I was. Rosa dear, please don't be that way. I think you have some nerve to talk to me that way when I am working my head off for you and the kids. I know you don't mean it.
Well dear, you are driving me crazy. I love you so much dear, I don't know what to do. I think so much of you that I have no desire for any one else but you. I will be home this week-end and it won't be here too soon for me. I live for the good time we are going to have building our little home for you and the kids. Write often dear.

I love you. Bob xxx

March 12, 1931

My Dearest and Hannah and Thelma,

Well, my love, I have not heard from you this week. I suppose you are so busy you don't have time to write but I am sure you think of me in your spare moments. The Countess is here and she keeps me on the jump. I hope you are not as lonesome as I am. Take good care of yourself, my dear and get good and strong. And please write every day as I love to hear from you so much. I lost the address of the man that I bought the lot (Cedar Grove) from. Please send it at once so I can pay on it.

Love, your Daddy xxx

April 4, 1931

My Dearest,

Well dear, this is Saturday night. I walked to town and sent you some flowers. I hope you like them. I would love to be with you all Easter. The Count stayed here until four today. This has been a funny week to me, my dear. I sure hope to be home next week-end. So get ready for the old crank to arrive. I am sending checks out tonight paying bills. It seems as though that is all I do is pay out. Well, my love, your alimony is here and don't spend it all in one place. Write as often as usual.

As ever, your Daddy xxxx

April 5, 1931, Easter

Dearest in the world,

This is Sunday and I never was so lonesome in all my life. I hope you don't miss me like I do you. How are you all? I am looking forward to the weekend so I can be home for a day. Take care of yourself dear and don't get upset. I want you to be well. Eat good and drink plenty of milk. I will be home Saturday morning or maybe Friday night. I have been keeping books all day and I am hungry so I will eat, then sleep so I can do a good weeks work as I am anxious to get done. But they keep adding on more work. Love the kids for me and plenty for yourself.

As ever, your Daddy xxxx

April 14, 1931

My dear Pug-nose,

How are you all? I have had some day. The men all quit and I have been out after others. I feel sure by this weekend I will have a new gang and everything going OK. I will pay $7.00 a week. Some difference in that and 12.00. I will also work nine hours Saturday and Sunday. Well, dear, I paid the gas bill that I brought with me. Mr. Baum and the Count will be here a week from this Friday. I will try and write every day. Remember me to Ma and love the kids for me and keep plenty for yourself for you are the dearest little girl in the world.

As ever, your Daddy. xxx

April 15, 1931

My Dearest,

I have not heard from you today. Please write. Well, I have a new crew on the job. I have been hanging canvas all day. I hung 62 square yards today. More extra work coming on the job. I am glad to be so busy. I have all I can do for some time yet so be a good girl and we will live in our own home this year. Well, dear, I won't need much rocking tonight.

As ever, your loving Daddy xxxx

April 28,1931

My Love,

Was so glad to hear from you and to know you are well. I am looking for you. I would like so much for you to stay with me for awhile. At least until you get tired of me. I would call you up more often but it cost so much. Please bring some thread and needles to sew some buttons on my clothes. Well dear, I am lonesome for you and the kids. Come right to the job when you come. Hoping mother is feeling good and tell her to rest.

As ever, your Daddy xxxx

May 1, 1931

Dearest in the world,

I went and got a haircut. I will have a good bath and go to bed. The waxing machine comes today. Today is the first of May. Just think I will be 33 years old this month. (May 25). I feel as though we were just married. I am sure you look younger now than 12 years ago. I am trying to be nice so you will put some buttons on my shirts.

Love to all. Your daddy xxxx

This is the last of 28 letters. At first I felt they were too personal for others to read. However, they do give insight into a young couple who shared difficult times, yet looked forward to building a future together.

Welcome to the Clan

Dad was busy finishing a project at Cà d' Zan, preparing to leave Florida, and thinking about a celebration for their fiftieth anniversary. All this going on, and he made time to write two letters to a very sick son-in-law.

Feb. 9, 1969

Dear John,

I don't feel a bit sorry for anyone that can find comfort and peace in this world and still be alive. How lucky can one get? I understand after four weeks you can go home and rest four more. Take a fool's advice and stay where you are the eight weeks. Especially if you have those candy-stripers waiting on you and good looking nurses caring for you. What a racket.

I went over to the East Coast fishing with my brother, Arthur. We got several large king fish. The sea was rough but lots of fun. We are both well, considering. I don't miss much in this world. Nothing like being prepared for the next one. I understand the Baptist have air conditioned Hell so it don't make much difference where one goes, providing one has friends in both places. If you could get the doctor to keep Thelma home and send you to Florida, you would soon be on the road to good health. Florida sunshine and lots of fruit and rest. I really mean it.

Rosa joins me in wishing you good health soon. Best to you, John
Pop Webb

On February 16, 1969, John received a second letter.

Dear John,

Thanks for your card. I am pleased you are still here. Now that you have been in the Webb family over twenty-five years, including all your headaches, heartaches and a would-be-heart attack, as Old Henry the Eighth would say, you are now a member of the Crown of Webb Royalty, with privilege to wear the Garter of Royalty. May your head stay off the block. Now that you have earned your way, far be it for me to drop the ax. We all have problems. I went to the bank last Tuesday. While there I met an old friend, now a vice president. He asked me to come in his office which I did. We had a couple and talked of the old days. I must of been gone at least 3 hours. Rosa called the bank and they could not find me. I was in a private office, having a ball. Someone must of called the police. I went out into the parking area of the bank and a cop that looked like a Martian with helmet and guns said, "Are you Bob Webb?" I said "Yes."

"Follow me."

I did. He took me right to where I lived and pointed to my house and never stopped. Right away I knew you had croaked. I went in the house. Rosa was eating cookies and looking at TV.

She said, "Where have you been? I was worried." It seems like the cops are kept busy leading old men home. What interested me was the cop just pointed.

So think yourself damn lucky you are in one place where we all know where you are. Stay there as long as you can because there is no peace outside and take care of yourself. Give my love to your nurse.

Welcome to the clan, Pop

Remembered by Others

*Mr. Webb used to do it all.
Everything.*

Bob Webb Making Bread

To gather information, I contacted a number of people who had worked for Dad at the various projects at Colonial Williamsburg. Most I had never met, a few I had heard of, and only Floyd Martin and Shorty did I know well. One interview led to another.

Bruce Wildenberger

Bruce Wildenberger, the first person I interviewed, was well prepared. All I had to do was plug in the tape recorder, relax, enjoy his wife's cookies, and let him tell his stories.

I went to work for Colonial Williamsburg in April, 1951. I walked in the old paint shop and asked who I'd see about getting a job, and they referred me back to your father. He questioned me about what kind of experience I had, where I was from, and this kind of thing, and after the discussion he said, "Well, if you come in Monday morning we wear white overalls, white shirt, white cap, a duster, putty knife, screw driver, sand paper and that's the standard uniform. Everybody wears it. I expect you to be here for inspection Monday morning."

So every Monday morning we used to have to go to the paint shop for roll call and inspection to make sure we had the proper white clothes on. Everything was white. He kinda gave everybody who worked for him the impression that he was a hard man to get along with, that he had come down from New Jersey to straighten things out in the paint shop.

I remember the first project I worked on, probably hadn't been working over ten days. It was the Chisel House. I was painting the stairway down to the basement, and of course I had my duster in my hip pocket. It had a long handle and I neglected to cut the handle off. So I had painted down one wall and turned around and kinda squatted to paint some on the other wall. The duster handle slid down the other wall and left a streak in it. About that time Mr. Webb walked in and said, "That's right, put it on and wipe it off, put it on and wipe it off." That was the way he usually handled the situation.

Another occasion when he visited the job, as he walked in he could hear these step ladders upstairs moving around, sliding across the floor, and of course his comment was, "I'm on to those old tricks. I know what you're doing. You're standing around waiting till you see me come, then you start moving the ladders around. I'm on to that, you can't pull that on me anymore."

So that was my first experience with your Dad.

The next experience I had with him, I guess it was two or three years later probably, he sent myself and this Harold McCandlish down to Bassett Hall to do some painting. Of course, we were using the paint that your Dad had come up with, the formulas he come with was lead paint, and the odd thing about that was, you put the paint on and it seemed to change color after it started drying. Of course everything was done by numbers, all the paints had different numbers. That way you identified the paint.

So McCandlish and myself went down to Bassett Hall to do some painting in a pantry down there and Mr. O'Neal, John O'Neal, who was at that time mixing colors, sent the paint down and put labels on the buckets with paint numbers. So we went ahead, I was acting leader on the job, so I mixed the paint and we got the walls all painted and went back to get the trim color. When I opened up the bucket of trim color and looked at it, I went back in and checked the walls. The walls were supposed to be light, the trim color dark, but the walls were much darker than the trim color according to the numbers on the bucket. So I went to the telephone and called the paint shop and your dad answered the phone and I said, "Mr. Webb, this is Wildenberger. We're down at Basset Hall, and they sent us the wrong color."

He said, "What?"

I said, "We put the color on the walls and it was supposed to go on the trim."

"Oh my God!" he said, "Hey John, there's some Burger on the phone, some kind of Burger, Hamburger, or something that wants to talk to you."

He couldn't remember my name, or he may have done it deliberately, but anyhow that's one of the incidents I remember.

Another one with Bassett Hall, at a later time, he sent me and McCandlish down. We were supposed to put some canvas on the ceiling. So we got down there and we put the canvas on, there was a shiny surface on it. After we got it all on, he come down and looked around, "My God what are all those little bubbles up there?"

"Well," I said, "that's water, Mr. Webb."

"We can't have that. We got to get somebody out there to get it out. That stuff will dry. I don't think that's going to come out right."

"Well, all I can tell you is my dad taught me when you put canvass on the wall if you get it on smooth, leave it, because eventually it will dry out." This was on a Friday.

He said, "Well, I hope so."

Sometime over the weekend something happened to the heating system at Bassett Hall and temperatures went up to the eighties, high eighties, low nineties. When we went back there Monday morning, it had dried and was stretched good and tight up there. So I was right proud of that. Of course, he didn't have any comments about that, no comments.

Your dad and I went up to Mr. Chorley's [president of Williamsburg Restoration] place up in New Jersey [Hopewell]. I went up there a couple of times, did some work. This one time we were going to put simulated white wash on a new addition Mr. Chorley put on his house.

We were staying in the gardener's house, they had a little addition on the gardener's cottage. A little room with a private bath, a little kitchenette in it, and we were staying in that. We were there probably between two and three weeks. We went out into this new room and got the walls ready with simulated whitewash that involved real heavy paint with putty whitening in it. I'd brush it on, then your dad would come along with the whisk broom and rough it, trying to make it look like whitewash. Of course it was a messy job. We were all covered with paint. One of the conditions of Mr. Webb going there was for Mr. Chorley to keep some beer in the refrigerator for him. Your Dad liked his beer now and then. So we went in there this one day to finish the ceiling. It was a big ceiling, the room was probably 16 feet wide and 24 feet long. It was quite a chore getting it done. We got it all finished, and your dad said, 'I sure could use a beer.'

So I went out to the room where they had the refrigerator where we were staying and got a beer for him and brought it in. He stood there in the middle of the room and popped the cap and when he did, it went swish! We didn't see anything then and went and ate supper. We walked back out there in the room so he could admire the work we had done. He look up on the ceiling, and here's about two dozen brown spots. Of course his comment was, "My God. What the hell is it?"

I said, "The only thing I can think of, Mr. Webb, was when you opened that can of beer it splattered on the ceiling."

"You think that's what it is?"

"It's gotta be. It's the only thing I can think of."

"Give me a damp rag real quick."

I rushed out and got him a damp rag, and he got up on the ladder and he was very carefully, just barely touching the ceiling with the damp rag. He got all those spots off. He got down off the ladder and looked up. "Looks all right now, don't it?"

"Yes it does."

"Well, let that be a lesson to you."

Later on during that period of time I began to get a little insight as to just what kind of character Mr. Webb was. We were sitting there one evening in the room. He'd had a few beers. I don't know if he was a little mellow or not but after he'd had two or three beers he commented, "Took me a long time to do it, but I think I finally have a good crew now. I think we have a good bunch of people down there."

He was kind of sentimental about it, and it really surprised me because I was used to the rough character, where nothing was right...nothing was ever right. But that always impressed me, the fact he said that.

Then he said, "Don't tell the guys down there I said that."

Oh, yes, there was one other time I remember when your dad did expose his temper. It was an incident when we were at the Motor House. We had this young fellow from over at Gloucester who wanted a job. We put him to work, but he just wasn't a painter. What it ended up was we had to tell him he was laid off. He didn't appreciate that, he was very unhappy about that. He thought he was doing his job like he should be.

To lead up to what happened, at that time down at the warehouse on occasion they would have some salvage material, and you could go over and buy it and take it home with you. And your dad had gone over and bought some salvage lumber and had it hauled out to his house. This young fellow knew something about your dad hauling lumber out there, so when he found out he was going to be laid off he went to the personnel office and told them up there, "I know that Mr. Webb was stealing lumber. I saw him haul some out to his house. A whole truckload he hauled out to his house."

And of course as soon as he left, the personnel office called down to talk to your dad about it, and the next thing I know he and John O'Neal come riding up in that pickup truck John used to drive. They slid to a stop in front of the building. Your dad got out and went to the foreman who was Milton Beverly at the time.

"Where's that SOB?"

Milton said, "Who's that?"

"That guy, the one from Gloucester."

Milton said, "He's right in here."

Your dad walked in, he was in one of the bathrooms painting a window, "Hey, come out here. Put anything that belongs to the company right there on that table and get your butt in the truck and get off this property right now. Don't you hang around here one second. You get off here right now before I have you put in jail."

Man, the guy came off, he didn't know what to say. He left in a hurry. Your dad was fuming, I tell you he was really fuming. Somebody had accused him of stealing lumber. He had gone in the warehouse and paid for it and knew he had done that. That's what upset him very much.

Now, in the paint shop there was a young fellow who came to work there. His name was Philip Moore, he was just a kid. Your dad used to do the coat of arms on the Palace, whenever that had to be done, and the pictorial work. Mr. Webb did it one time and the second time, this young fellow, Philip Moore, a born artist, went out to help your dad. He worked with your dad for some time on that coat of arms. He's still working at the paint shop–he's the artist.

Harold West, and another fellow they hired later, rode a bicycle with baskets over the front wheel. They'd put in a bucket of water, soap, sponges. And they had a mixture of linseed oil and turpentine and they'd go out along the street and wash all the low parking signs, stop signs, all the signs that were low along the street...not the pictorial signs, but all the other signs. They'd take soap and water and wash them all off, then they'd dry them. Then take the linseed oil and vinegar...beg your pardon, that's what it was, linseed oil and vinegar, that mixture. They'd wipe it on the signs and wipe it dry and that would rejuvenate the paint. That would make them last that much longer and they wouldn't have to be painted so often. That was one of the things your dad come up with.

Of course he came up with that Williamsburg paint–1..2..3–that was the numbers on it. Each one was a little different formula. He had a formula book there with all these formulas in it and every time we made a paint we had to come make it up according to that formula.

Basically, when I went there everything they were using as far as paint was concerned was lead and oil. The interior paint, they would take the lead and wash all the linseed oil out of it and put flattening oil in it for flat paint and then they'd use lead mixing oil for enamel and use sipes enamel oil, that's how they'd make the gloss. Of course, it was hard paint to handle. You'd get a little heavy spot and it would start to run and when you were painting doors you had to paint out each panel then wipe all the edges and paint around the panel. If you left anything on, it would lap up and show laps, and with a double coat on it would look different. Oh, it was rough stuff to use.

The Pittsburgh Paint Company had the right to duplicate the paint color. The paint they made the colors with was not the paint we used. We used lead and oil paint. They were making it out of standard ingredients which is probably a lot of calcium carbonate and zinc oxide. Those kind of fillers. We made up our paints out of lead and different colors in oil or colors in Japan. The interior paints were basically color in Japan, they dry much quicker.

Japan is a liquid that goes into the paint. Just where it comes from, I'm not sure, I never researched just where Japan comes from but that's the name for the liquid.

I interrupted to ask about Charley George, the black, one-armed secretary Dad hired at a time when blacks worked mostly as laborers. Remarks were made and Dad's answer was, "The man can do the job. He has a family to support. So that's that!"

Charley George? I didn't know him. Most of my time spent there was not around the shop itself. After I worked a short while I became a lead man on the job with three other painters and we used to have to call our time in at night. I may have talked to Charley on the telephone but his job there was basic, as was all the clerks, they kept a complete record of every portion of a building, what kind of paint was used on it, when it was painted last and how many coats of paint we put on, the whole works. We had five filing cabinets down there just for the records. That was another thing your dad instituted, keeping a complete record of every job, every color, and so on.

When I first went to work there I worked on some new construction to start with, then after they got that pretty well caught up we went back into repainting the oldest buildings and everything was duplicated. The same paint color was put back on every time we repainted.

Your father was very organized. Another thing he instituted was a board. In the paint shop we had this pile of panels with hooks on it. Then we had wooden chips made about two-and-a-half inches wide and three-and-a-half inches long, and all these paint colors would be painted on a wooden chip and on the back would be the formula, the colors used in it. These were hung on the board and every time we made a new batch of paint we had to go and get a chip off and add the ingredients to mix the color.

And then we had a board there that was painted flat black with two holes in it side-by-side and on the back of the board a door opened, and on the back of the door were a couple of hooks there. And what you did was after you made the color on a wooden chip you hung the original over behind one of those black holes and your sample on the other one. Then you had to get an architect to come down to look at it to approve whether or not that was matching. That was before technology came in where you'd put it in a machine that would tell you whether it matched or not. That was the system we used. It worked reasonably well.

As paint ages it gradually gets grayer. You have to take the gray out to get back to the original color, so that's why the biggest majority of Williamsburg colors are soft or muted colors. They weren't sharp color like they have now. Those paints had to have just a touch of raw umber to knock off that sharpness to give that soft look.

The way they developed the original Williamsburg colors was they would go out into the field to an original house and they'd take paint remover and select a spot on the wood work somewhere and remove that paint one layer at a time till they got down to the last coat, the first coat next to the wood and they'd determine whether or not that was a prime coat or whether that was a finish color. Then they'd go into the field with all these different colors and sit there and mix the color and match it to that particular color that they found. There were 24 basic colors that they found to start off with.

That's what Pittsburgh started duplicating, if I'm not mistaken. I can't verify it but it was 24 or 36, one of the two. A lot of the colors Pittsburgh sold were what we call let-downs. They'd take a basic color, and what I mean by let-down is, they had a formula where they took the original color and added so many parts of white to it and this would lighten it up and they had a formula of two-to-one, four-to-one, eight-to-one. Of course the eight-to-one would be real light, and you'd put that on the ceilings, then maybe the four to one would go on the walls and the original color would go on the woodwork. That's how many of the rooms were painted out there, in that fashion. But your dad was one of these people who would formulate these colors to match those samples.

When they removed the building or sometimes when they restored a building they'd take the lumber off, a door trim or something, and bring it into the shop and it would be stripped down to the original color and be matched in the shop.

At one time there they were using what I call patent paint, and this was where the paint company would manufacture the paint and you would add color to it, whatever color you want. But as I understand it, when your dad came he started using the basic lead–basic white lead–and all the colors were made from that except the real dark colors. The real dark colors were made with those colors of Japan that I talked about earlier. They would take that and add sipes enamel oil to make the enamel or flattening oil to make a flat paint. That's how we got the real dark colors that went on shutters and doors and that kind of thing. He basically came up with all these formulas.

There's a story there somewhere, I heard a little about but I don't know just how it worked out. It seems when your dad first got there they had someone there making paint colors and for some reason, I don't know just what happened, but as I understood it, your dad and this fellow got into a disagreement and the fellow demanded something and if he didn't get it he was going to quit.

So your dad said, "Good-bye." That's when he took over and started making all the colors himself. I think shortly after they had John O'Neal come in assisting in making colors, he gradually become what we call the color man.

Then John became shop foreman and then superintendent when your dad left. I remember out on a job you'd see the pick-up truck coming and here is John driving and your dad sitting over there on the passenger side looking and taking everything in. He loved it, but some of the men used to hate it when he came out on the job because he always had some kind of comment to make. Always something that wasn't quite right, not quite like it was supposed to be. Of course, he could pass out a compliment–not often–but you knew you well deserved it.

The union came in one time and tried to organize the whole maintenance departments. The biggest majority of the carpenters belonged to the union, I don't remember the paint department being involved with any union. The question of union never came up while he was there.

Basically when I went to work there in '51, I went to work out in the field. In '54 they sent me up with three other fellows to Merchant Square. I was called the lead man. I was the one to get to do the extra work, get the paint out, get it all ready, make sure things were done right. Then when they started to build the motor house in the mid '50s, I went out there and I was foreman of the paper-hanging crew. We put the material on the walls and that kind of thing. In the '60's, when your dad retired, I made assistant superintendent. John O'Neal became superintendent.

During your dad's tenure at Colonial Williamsburg, their criteria was that time and money were not important. It had to be done right. Period. That's the way I was taught. If you do the job right, people will forget the cost, but you do a bad job, it's never forgotten.

That was one thing that used to bother him. On some of the construction jobs...the Goodwin building which was headquarters...for some unknown reasons they decided everything should be done on the same day. All the carpenter work should be finished on the same day as the painting. Now, this is just not very practical, it's impossible. So what they would do, we would start to work on a room and then say, okay, this room is ready. So we'd go in the next and here's electricians snaking wires and scratching the walls we just painted.

They'd say, "What are you complaining about? Those three walls are all right, this is the only one you got to paint again."

Your dad used to just jump up and down when they would pull something like that.

Mr. Hacket was general manager. He came in on the job one day and somebody was doing something there he didn't think was right, so he told them to stop. The foreman went back to Mr. Webb and told him what this man had said.

"Where's he now?"

"Over there on the job."

He got in the truck and said, "Let's go."

He went over there to Mr. Hacket, "Look, when my men are on the job they report to me. I don't want you coming here telling them anything. If you've got anything you want them to know you come and tell me. I'll tell them."

And that's just the way he talked, "You keep your nose out of my business. If you want something changed, you come and tell me, and I'll go and tell them to change it."

He was loyal to his men.

Bob Webb's Colonial Williamsburg Paint Crew
Photo courtesy of Colonial Williamsburg

This fellow was deaf and mute and had a brother working here, too. This fellow was touch-up man. He had a motorized scooter with all the different colors. If somebody removed a picture and put a little hole in the wall, he'd go out and patch it and touch it up to match the existing wall. His name was Horace Medley.

This fellow here, I worked with him on two or three jobs, he got me in big trouble. We went to the Deane House to put up scenic wallpaper. He was doing the pasting and trimming, and I was doing the hanging. That was another job your dad bailed me out of. We put a light-weight fabric, like cheesecloth, on the wall, so if they wanted to take the scenic paper off, they'd have something to take it off with. We had no problem with that. Then we started hanging the scenic. Of course, the top portion had no paint on it, and the bottom part had all this heavy paint on it. So as we pasted, where there was paint it hardly moved at all, but where there was no paint the paper would either shrink or expand. When he went to trim it, instead of getting a nice straight edge...I'm trying to butt it edge-to-edge, without overlapping. When I finally get it up there to slide it over for a butt joint, the cheesecloth would get damp from the paste and slide over with it. When it dried, I had a lot of hair-like cracks in the joint, and Mr. Webb came in and looked at that.

"What happened up there?"

I said, "Evidently the lining underneath it got wet and shrank a little bit."

"Well, we'll have to see what we can do about that!"

He went back to the shop and sends the touch-up man. He [Horace Medley] gets up there with his artist brushes and paints the little cracks to match the paper.

That's when he bailed me out. Mr. Webb was a good ol' fellow...just a dry wit about him.

On the art work, in duplicating various signs, they made what is called a punch pattern. This is a piece of paper with little tiny holes which outlined each design. Then they have a record to tell which color goes where. What you do is take this punch pattern, put it on whatever you are going to paint the design on, and take a white powder tied in a soft cloth, and just pounce it. That leaves an outline where your pattern is supposed to go. Usually they have a photograph of the design to go by for fine details.

Your dad had the easy part because when he made colors there was no problem getting all the various colors in oil or in Japan. He could get any amount of any of the colors he wanted, so when you were ready to make a color you had everything available. But then after he left, all those colors gradually faded out. They no longer made any colors in Japan oil. You could no longer find any color in oil. All of a sudden, everything became chemical colors so all those colors had to be reformulated with chemical colors. So we had to go though the whole process all over again.

One of the things that did help us in reformulating the colors was that we had a color machine. There we could mix the colors, and we had color cards where we could set the formula, and as we made them we could punch out the formula on the cards. And we also had what is called a color eye, which is an electronic machine that measured the colors and would tell you what shade you are off. We had all this modern technology to help us make the colors, which your dad didn't have. Everything he made had to be done by eye.

The hard part for him was to match by eye, which is much more tolerant than what the machine is. The machine is much more exacting. It will tell you if it is off. With your eye it depends on the lighting. Artificial light is one color, you go out in natural light and it's another color. The secret there is knowing what to add to the color to get it to change to the shade you want.

You learn from somebody else. I learned from my dad. He did graining–he could marbleize–that's a lost art now. The old method was you had to learn from scratch how to do it. You had to have somebody show you how to do it. That's one of the lost arts. There are very few people in this country today who can actually marbleize and make it look authentic. Graining, my dad used to take a panel door and grain that thing and make it look like oak, knotty pine, whatever kind of wood, he could do it. I don't know how.

My dad was a paint contractor who could do all these things. So when I went to work for him as an apprentice I was only 18 years old. Altogether, when I came down here I had ten years experience in the painting trade–six as an apprentice, four as a painter.

I never took the time to learn how to grain or how to marbleize. My older brother did, he did those things.

Mr. Webb was going to Sarasota to do some graining down there, but he didn't have any combs. I said, "I think my brother has combs."

He said, "Can I borrow them?"

I said, "I think so."

Combs are in a metal box about a half-inch thick, four-inches square. In this are all these thin, metal sheets with long teeth with little slots cut in them, some were very narrow, some were wider. What you do is put your background on, then put the stain on, then you drag the combs down through the stain. That's what gives you the grain in the wood. By swirling a little bit and using different combs, it gives you the different texture in the grain.

My dad used to spend hours taking the old, rubber rollers off wringer washers and cutting them about four inches long. Then he'd take a pocket knife and cut out the design and leave the eye that you sometimes see in the maple or the oak. By taking that thing and by rolling and dragging it a little bit at the same time, you'd get the wider grain. I saw all that as a kid, but I never did it.

The visit with Bruce was enjoyable and led me to others who had worked with Bob.

Verlin Hubbard

The afternoon spent with Verlin Hubbard was special. I knew Dad saw himself in the lad who quit school, left the Kentucky mountains, and lied about his age hoping to be hired. The boy didn't know he was opening himself to lessons that would guide him throughout his life.

Dad gave Hubbard a job and a chance to learn a trade at the age of 17, just as Lamb had done for him. Later, after Verlin married he lived on Webb's Acre.

I went there when I was seventeen. I didn't finish school in the mountains of Kentucky. I came out here and went to work and lied about my age. I told Mr. Webb I was nineteen. I lied so I could get the job. He hired me. He might have thought, "I'll give him a chance."

He had two little buildings in the back of his big house. I rented a cottage all the way in the back on the right. One time me and my ex-wife were having a little fuss. Mr. Webb walked up the driveway and took a two-by-four and hit the side of the house.

"Hush that mess in there."

It sounded like a gun went off out there. We quieted down. Then we walked out and seen him walking down the road, and he was laughing. Then we started laughing, too. He was a character!

Another time, Mr. Webb put me on restriction because of this argument me and the wife had. I had said something to him, and the wife, too, and he put me out there cleaning buckets for a week! Shorty was there, too. Then he finally let me back outside.

Shorty worked there in the paint shop Monday through Friday. He'd go out to the Webbs' on weekends and do yard work. I remember seeing Shorty a lot of times, practically every weekend he'd be doing something for Mr. Webb. His job during the week was keeping the paint shop clean, keeping it straightened up, keeping all the paint pots washed out and clean.

When he emptied the new paint out into where they mixed the paint, he'd do the bucket that the paint came in. We just used kerosene, that cleaned it. The paint was boiled linseed oil and lead, that's what it was. That's what we used there for a long time until they went to latex.

Dutch Boy had a regular oil you mixed with it, called lead mixing oil that they mixed with the paint. And that was the exterior paint but the inside paint was regular oil-based satin. I don't think that had as much lead in it.

Colonial Williamsburg started out with Dutch Boy, then they went to Pittsburgh, and now they're with Martin-Senour. During Mr. Webb's time, it was Pittsburgh that had the rights to the Williamsburg colors.

Bruce Wildenberger taught me to wallpaper, Bruce, John O'Neil and Mr. Webb. When I started doing some paper hanging Mr. Webb gave me his paper outfit. He gave me the cutting board, the straight edge, the rule...everything pertaining to paper hanging. He gave me the tools, all that. He was a super nice guy.

Mr. Webb did a lot of marbleizing in the Williamsburg Inn. It still looks super today. You drive around the front entrance. To the left is another big door. Right as you go in the East Lounge you'll see the marbleizing on a big door casing over the circular stairway. The baseboard, too. It stands out. I keep it touched up, washed up with mild soap and water. They've got a special soap we use.

There's marbleizing in the Abby Aldrich Rockefeller Folk Art Center. It's on the second floor. The C.W. guys still take care of it. I think people walk on it. It's still good because they go in there every so often and take care of it, clean it up and touch it up. Webb did a lot of work in there.

He used to do the carriages. He always painted them and striped them, pin-striped them with a brush by hand. Mr. Webb used to do it all. Everything. I think Ronnie Combs did the letters for him, but he did the striping himself. I've seen him do it.

The Inn furniture–it was all oak. We had to strip it down and put three coats of varnish on it. Then take steel wool and wax and rub it down until it got real smooth, a clear, slick finish like Mr. Webb wanted. We used a paste wax like simonize. We spent a lot of time like that. I'd go to him and ask him if it was okay and he'd say, "No!" I had to get a piece of steel wool and wax and rub it some more.

With Mr. Webb, quality was number one. And he believed in it, and he made sure it was right, too. Everybody, I don't care who it was, he'd have them in the office to talk about it. He saw that the job was done right. I swear he wouldn't compromise on quality. Maybe that's the reason he stayed as long as he did.

I worked there with them until '74 then I quit and went into business for myself. Now, I'm back doing stuff for Colonial Williamsburg. I've got myself and two other painters working for me.

I left Verlin smiling...Bob Webb, the mentor, lives on!

Philip Moore

I ignored the sign that read, "Private area. Employee personnel only" and opened the door to what had been Webb's paint shop and still is the paint shop.

Philip Moore was standing in front of a high table viewing pattern designs on large sheets of paper. I introduced myself and glanced at the designs, "These designs were punched with little holes?"

Phil replied, "No. Perforated."

"That's what you call it? I suppose those patterns are all gone."

Phil said, "No, they've got them in here that go back to the 1930s. The old blue ones. This one is 1950."

Mr. Webb retired in 1963, I think. I came here in '65. So I didn't actually work with him when he was supervisor of the paint shop, but I had been here less than a year, about six months, and the crafty old devil was doing the coat of arms up on the Capitol. It's on a piece of special plywood like five feet wide and ten feet high. It had to be ordered special because it is so big. It doesn't look that big down on the ground. So he goes to the architect department and he gets the pattern, the paper drawing of it, full size...ten feet high. Then he comes down here to John O'Neil [paint supervisor] and says, "Look, let me take the kid out there and show him a little something about how to do this." I was nineteen.

He knew exactly what he was doing. He got me out there in his studio, and for three days I punched that pattern out using a dowel with a nail in the end of it. So it was punch, punch, punch. It's out in the car, I've still got it. In those days, all you did was

---

take a little dowel and insert a nail in it and you sat there and you had a little piece of cardboard under the paper, so it would be soft under there. You sit there and it was punch, punch, punch, all around this English coat of arms. It took me about three days.

He was real nice. I think he fed me lunch while I was out there. He didn't have to do any pouncing of the pattern, I'll tell you! Anyway, he started painting. I stayed out there. After that I guess I mostly watched him. That was the last one he did. Then I started doing them after that.

He did all the pictorial signs, all the character separations, because the sign painters that were here before him may not have been capable of doing that artistic type of work. So anyway, I sort of was a natural at it, and I started doing it. Now I do all the pictorial signs.

The pattern signs are done the same way. Hand-painted letters and perforated patterns. Let me show you this perforator over here. Instead of using the dowel with the nail in the end of it... I was here for eight years and we got this little contraption, that would make it '73. This needle [looks like a pencil with a needle inserted at the end] is grounded on this metal plate, and you just draw it down the paper and it perforates. If you hold it just right, you can cut a piece out. From the point...through the paper...to the plate, and it will shock the living daylights out of you too. So that's what we use.

It would have saved me three days of hand-punching. But the funny thing about it, Mr. Webb was so particular, I'd sit there and punch on an angle, he'd say, "No, no, no. I want you to punch it straight down. I want a nice round hole, I don't want something going in on an angle."

That's all it was, drawing your patterns by hand, then punch away the little holes to outline it. A lot of days we'd spend the whole day just drawing patterns.

In the old days, letters came out the way the painter painted them. Everything is computerized now. There's still a great demand for the designs with the perforated outline. There's a lot of custom, hand-painted stuff, really fancy stuff. I'll tell you one thing, there's a lot of people now that's working in a sign shop that never pick up a brush. A young person comes into a sign shop and they start right off with a machine. They never had the experience of making letters with a brush, maybe one or two guys in a sign shop of ten people and they're the only ones who know how to paint with a brush.

The old method is more of an art now. You get more respect if you can letter with a brush. Young people in a sign shop now don't believe it can be done.

This vinyl is the actual letter that will go on a sign instead of the paint. Like striping on an automobile. You use the vinyl strips instead of painting the stripes with a brush. You can program to do line after line. You can do in a short time what it used to take days to do.

I tell you, Mr. Webb never saw anything like this. He'd have a fit. He'd say, "The country's gone to hell."

I worked with several sign painters. Elbert Dearing, he was the one I was apprenticed to, then there was Ronnie Combs. Years ago they had one here named George Franklin and a guy named Slater.

I laughed, "Yeah, Slater. I knew him. The forefinger on his right hand was amputated, and when he'd shake hands he'd take that stub and rub the palm of your hand. You'd only get caught once. He painted a number of signs on his own time and he'd sign them, 'Slater Did It.'

"When my sister was expecting her first baby, Slater's wife gave her a baby book and Slater signed it, 'Slater Did It.'

"Don't you find an advantage having come from the old system to this new system?"

Yes. The young people learning this art now don't have the advantage of knowing the old system. Sitting down drawing by hand I think helps with your layout better. Although you can do it on the screen.

On the pictorial signs we used the old, perforated patterns and did the lettering by hand. It's not very authentic to have the signs up there with vinyl letters on them. But we use it on almost everything else.

I remember the time your father went to Russia. He was retired, but he'd stop by every once in awhile, mostly when he wanted to get himself a brush or some sandpaper or something. He went to Russia at the height of the cold war, back in the '70s.

He was here one day and I said, "Man, what in the world do you want to go to Russia for?"

He said, "Hell, there ain't nothing wrong with those people over there. They're just like we are."

He was right. We get full of all this government propaganda, these evil people. I don't know why he ever chose to go to Russia.

He was a character!

The Williamsburg colors are done different now. Instead of going to the color chips that were for the color mixer to hand mix five gallons of paint at a time and to match the chip hanging on the wall–it's like the sign equipment–it's all computerized now. There's a paint machine back there, push the buttons and it matches the color you want.

The original chips are still there. The colors have changed after so many years. They've turned dark and gotten dirty. There's about twelve hundred over there.

The coaches–we still got all these old patterns for the carriages. I did the Landau Carriage. One of the nicest ones they have, and Mr. Webb was the last to do that. Golden color background. It had a little squirrel and coat of arms on it. We completely repainted and decorated it. And it had a C.A.A. [Carriage Association of America] on it. They've met here two times since I've been here. The last time was three years ago in Carter's Grove, and they had me go down to give a talk on decoration of the carriages. Gold leafing and things like that. They had a contest down there for "first place restoration competition." So the Landau Carriage won first place, and they brought the plaque down here and gave it to us. That was the first time it had been redone since your father did it. It was redone in l994. That's the one they don't use very much, so that lasted a long time.

The Mulberry, painted a real pretty maroon, and the blue one they have, and another one–they use those every day. All day long and wear them out almost every year. They come in here to be completely done over, so we've done those numerous times. But not the Laudau. That was the one they use to carry dignitaries.

We do the carriages now out in the shop. All the decorations and everything in the open room. Your father would never had put up with that! I mean never! He made a large area, hung drop cloths from the ceiling to the floor, with an overlapping area he could walk between. Then there were large pans of water on the floor with about an inch or two of water. If you had permission (God help you if you didn't) to go into this dust-protected area, you had to step in the pans of water often so your shoes wouldn't create or leave particles of dust.

He wrote a booklet one time of what is expected of the painters, how they were to dress. I remember one of the funny lines was, "The days of the itinerant painter are over. You will come to work in clean, white clothes, clean shaven, and with clean fingernails" and all that.

He had Monday-morning inspection. He was a stickler for cleanliness. No doubt about that!

He hired a painter from Norge. He'd been in the Merchant Marines in W.W. II. He always had a grudge against your Dad 'cause when he came here he had a misunderstanding. The first thing on his job, he went to the hardware store...I think he misunderstood your father...he went there and he bought his own sandpaper to come here to sand in the shop. Webb said, 'Dumb fool, you don't buy your own sandpaper! You get it here.'

He said, "Okay. How about giving me my money back?"

Your father wouldn't give him the money back. He was a character!

I think he ran the place with an iron hand. He actually got me interested in the art work I do. It's hard for me to paint here all day, then go home and paint. I don't have a studio or easel set-up. I've done all kinds of pictures. I'm really good at copying stuff. I can copy, but to create it myself is a little hard.

I remember how impressed I was when I went out there [Webb's Acre]. He had little rental properties with signs on them, the Barn, the Studio, the Cottage, and the Wheelhouse. A real artist studio–and I believe he had a skylight facing the north light, what a true artist is supposed to paint by. He had stuff all in the house. I was really impressed. Big easel. Matter of fact, he told me if anything ever happened to him to come out there and try to buy that easel.

I smiled, "I have that easel. It was given to him by Colonial Williamsburg as a retirement present. It has a brass plaque engraved with his name and his date of retirement, November 30, 1962. I gave it to his grandson and namesake."

Tramp Artist: The Life of Robert Webb

Final Words

Goodnight and God bless you.

Bob and Tippy

W hen Dad was in his eighties I asked, "How does a cane help you?" His answer was, "If you live long enough, you'll find out."

I have now lived long enough. And I now use his cane.

Writing Dad's biography has been a nine-year endeavor that has led to many adventures. During this time, I grew in understanding and love for a complex, undefeatable, self-made man.

As a child ready for bed, my father always said to me, "Goodnight and God bless you." As a young adult leaving home to go into my own life, he said, "Take care of yourself, and God bless you." As an older adult, sharing our last hours together, he said, "God bless you."

...and to Dad, "God did bless me when He gave me you for my father."

Tramp Artist: The Life of Robert Webb

Ripples in the Pool

T his chapter provides some of the important pages from Bob Webb's life. Obviously, it is not a complete collection; yet, a few of the important documents are included. Bob's life, like anyone else's, is an aggregate of details. Often these details seem disparate, but–ultimately–they are all interconnected.

Awards for Work at Williamsburg

For his excellent service to Colonial Williamsburg, Dad received several awards, some of which appear in this section.

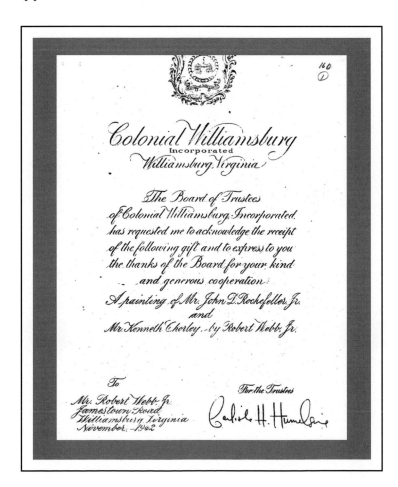

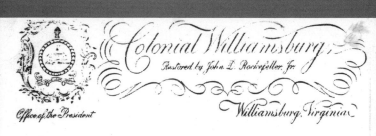

Office of the President

Williamsburg, Virginia

November 30, 1962

Dear Bob:

It is virtually impossible for me to say exactly how much your supervision of the Colonial Williamsburg paint program has meant to all of us involved in the work of this organization. As you well know, I am especially reminded of the standards of excellence and high achievement in paint work every day that I live in the Norton-Cole House. The examples that come to mind are far too numerous to list, but the marbleized floor on the porch is one thing that continues to give pleasure and enjoyment to everyone who views it. Beyond that, the paint work, both practical and decorative, and the pictorial signs throughout the restored area are always works of high competence and artistic achievement.

I am glad to have this opportunity to send you this expression of my appreciation and warmest congratulations for a job well done. I am particularly pleased to know that we will still have the opportunity in the future, from time to time, to call on you for special assignments and work on particular projects where your own skills and artistry will be especially useful.

It is my hope that the future years will hold an abundance of happiness and good health. Accept, as always, my best wishes.

Sincerely,

Carlisle H. Humelsine

Mr. Robert Webb, Jr.
Route 1, Box 82
Jamestown Road
Williamsburg, Virginia

And I especially want to add a personal note of thanks and appreciation for your many,

Tramp Artist: The Life of Robert Webb

Architects Give Webb Top Award

Robert Webb Jr., of Williamsburg, was presented the distinguished Master Craftsman Award in the field of architectural painting at the annual awards banquet of the Virginia Chapter of the American Institute of Architects in the Virginian Hotel Friday night.

Webb was honored for his restoration of Colonial Williamsburg paintings.

* * *

Webb, winner of the Master Craftsman Award, has served since May 1940 as superintendent of all painting work required in the restoration of the historic buildings of Williamsburg and for the hotels and other commercial buildings owned and operated by Colonial Williamsburg.

* * *

HE PERSONALLY executed the pictorial signs that identify the shops and taverns in the 18th century manner. He also painted the coats-of-arms, shields and emblems appearing on the governor's palace, the capitol and some of the other larger buildings in and adjacent to the historic area.

A native of Massachusetts, he served in the Navy in World War I as a camouflage artist in the Fifth Naval District. He was long associated with the well-known artist John Singer Sargent and worked on some of the notable murals in the Boston Public Library.

Richmond Times-Dispatch, Sunday, May 6, 1962 C-9

Virginia Architects Honor Local Firms

Robert Webb Jr. of Williamsburg was presented the distinguished master craftsman award in the field of architectural painting at the meeting of the Virginia chapter of the American Institute of Architects yesterday in Lynchburg.

DAILY PRESS, Newport News, Va., Wed., May 9, 1962   15

WILLIAMSBURG, JAMES CITY COUNTY

Webb Receives Craftsmanship Award For State

WILLIAMSBURG—Robert Webb superintendent of paint work for Colonial Williamsburg, Inc., has received an award "for high standards and recognized skill as a master craftsman in the field of architectural painting" from the Virginia chapter of the American Institute of Architects.

Webb, who has supervised painting at the Colonial Restoration since 1940, has personally executed dozens of pictorial signs which identify shops and taverns throughout the restored area, as well as painted ornamental coats-of-arms, shields and emblems on buildings such as the capitol and the Governor's Palace and colonial carriages.

The craftsman is a native of Massachusetts who started his career in Boston in the studio of F. M. Lamb, an associate of John Singer Sargent. During World War I he was a camouflage artist and after the war he worked in Florida, where he did all the interior decoration at Sarasota's John Ringling Museum, and in several Eastern cities before joining the staff of Colonial Williamsburg.

VIRGINIA CHAPTER

THE AMERICAN INSTITUTE OF ARCHITECTS

REPLY TO: Goodwin Building, Williamsburg, Virginia

160
10

April 27, 1962

Mr. Robert Webb, Jr.
Jamestown Road
Williamsburg, Virginia

Dear Bob:

On behalf of the Virginia Chapter of the American Institute of
Architects, I have the honor and pleasure of extending to you and Mrs. Webb
a cordial invitation to attend a reception and banquet to be held at The
Virginian Hotel, Lynchburg, Virginia, on Friday, May 4, 1962, at 6:00 p.m.
The banquet will be the principal event of this Annual Spring meeting of
the Chapter.

At this affair, honor awards are going to be presented to two members
of our Chapter for outstanding public service and service to the Chapter.
Furthermore, you have been selected to receive an award for outstanding craftsmanship in the field of Architectural Painting, so another feature of the meeting
will be its presentation to you.

I regret deeply that a long planned trip to the Midwest to consult
on a new important restoration project will make it impossible for Mrs. Kendrew
and me to meet and be with you and Mrs. Webb at Lynchburg on this occasion.
However, I am glad to say that your friends, Ernie and Nannie Frank, will be
there and would like to meet you at the reception at 6:00 p.m. at The Virginian
Hotel and attend the banquet with you. Mr. Fleming Hurt, the President of the
Virginia Chapter, is looking forward to greeting you. Mr. A. O. Budina, Vice-
Chairman of our Committee, will meet you too, and advise you of any details
concerning the presentation.

A room has been reserved for you at The Virginian for Friday night,
and it is hoped that you and Mrs. Webb will stay over and enjoy the features
and lovely countryside of that area on Saturday.

I will appreciate the early receipt of your acceptance of this invitation.

With hearty congratulations to you and deep pride in your many contri-
butions to the architectural success of so many buildings in Virginia and other
states, and again with regret that I cannot witness the presentation of this
award to you,

Sincerely,

A. Edwin Kendrew
Chairman
Committee on Awards and Scholarships

Glimpses of Cà d' Zan

This chapter provides photographs of work that Bob Webb performed at Cà d' Zan on the John Ringling estate in Sarasota Florida.

Renovations Underway
Photo by Geoffrey Steward

Ceiling Details
Photos by Jay Wright

Bathroom Views

Green Bathroom

Photos by Giovanni Lunardi

Yellow Bathroom

Pink Bathroom
Photos by Giovanni Lunardi

Panels

Foyer Panel

Mable's Bathroom

Ceiling under Balcony

Photos by Terry Schank

Glimpses of Williamsburg

T his chapter provides photographs of work that Bob Webb performed for the Colonial Williamsburg Foundation in Williamsburg, Virginia.

Signage

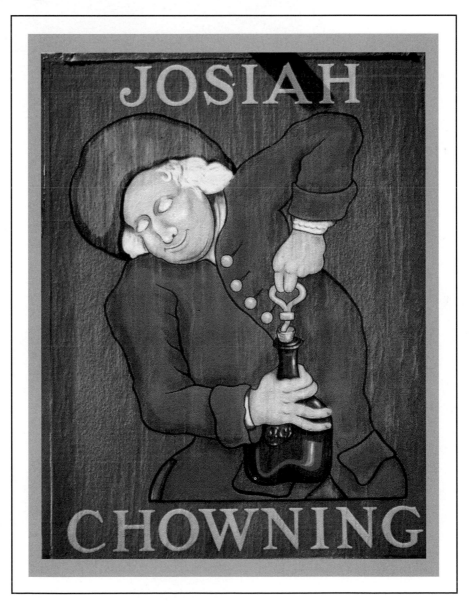

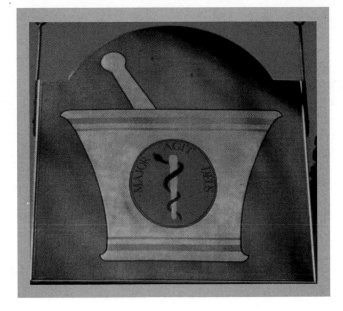

Carriages and Heraldry

Arms of Great Britain

Wythe Chariot

Glimpses of Other Projects

This chapter provides photographs of work that Bob Webb performed for various projects in America.

Riverside Baptist Church

The following pictures are from the roof beams and heraldic borders located in the Riverside Baptist church in Jacksonville, Florida.

Photo credit: Gunnar Miller

Bellamy United Methodist Church

The following pictures are from the mural, "Suffer the Little Children To Come unto Me" located in Bellamy United Methodist church in Gloucester, Virginia.

Photo credits:
Michael W. Teagle

Landscapes and Still Lifes

The following pictures Bob painted for his own enjoyment. He was equally comfortable painting large murals and small canvases.